YOUR CHILD
AT PLAY

Five to Eight Years

Volumes in the
Your Child at Play Series

~~~~~~~~~~~~~~~

YOUR CHILD AT PLAY:
Birth to One Year—Discovering the Senses
and Learning About the World

YOUR CHILD AT PLAY:
One to Two Years—Exploring, Learning,
Making Friends, and Pretending

YOUR CHILD AT PLAY:
Two to Three Years—Growing Up,
Language, and the Imagination

YOUR CHILD AT PLAY:
Three to Five Years—Conversation, Creativity,
and Learning Letters, Words, and Numbers

YOUR CHILD AT PLAY:
Five to Eight Years—Building Friendships,
Expanding Interests, and Resolving Conflicts

IN TIME AND WITH LOVE:
Caring for the Special Needs Baby
—Birth to Three Years

YOUR CHILD AT PLAY

Five to Eight Years

Building Friendships, Expanding Interests,
and Resolving Conflicts

MARILYN SEGAL, PH.D.,
AND BETTY BARDIGE, ED.D.

Foreword by Samuel J. Meisels, Ph.D.,
School of Education, University of Michigan

A "Your Child at Play" Series Book

NEWMARKET PRESS   NEW YORK

To our children

The authors gratefully acknowledge the A. L. Mailman Family Foundation, Inc., for their support of the photographs of this book.

All royalties earned on the sales of Your Child at Play *are contributed to the Family Center of Nova Southeastern University.*

This is a Mailman Family Center Book, published by Newmarket Press, drawn from research conducted at Nova Southeastern University, Ft. Lauderdale, Florida.

10   9   8   7   6   5   4   3   2   1

Library of Congress Cataloging-in-Publication Data

Segal, Marilyn.
    Your child at play: Five to eight years: building friendships, expanding interests, and resolving conflicts / Marilyn Segal and Betty Bardige: foreword by Samuel J. Meisels.
       p.   cm.
    Includes index.
    1. Play—United States.   2. Child development—United States.   I. Bardige, Betty Lynn Segal. II. Title.
    HQ782.S4255   1999
    305.231—dc21   99-42101
ISBN 1-55704-402-3 (hc.)   CIP
ISBN 1-55704-401-5 (pbk.)

QUANTITY PURCHASES
Companies, professional groups, clubs, and other organizations may qualify for special terms when ordering quantities of this title. For information, write to Special Sales, Newmarket Press, 18 East 48th Street, New York, NY 10017; call (212) 832-3575; fax (212) 832-3629; or e-mail newmktprs@aol.com.

www.newmarketpress.com

PHOTO CREDITS:
LISA NALVEN PHOTOGRAPHY: pp. 6, 8, 9, 13, 19, 25, 34, 36 (bottom), 36 (top), 39, 59, 60, 62, 63, 64 (top), 69, 72, 75, 76, 78, 96, 101, 102 (top and bottom), 103, 108 (bottom), 108 (top), 110, 114, 132, 134, 149, 152, 153, 155, 157, 159 (left), 159 (right), 160, 162, 170, 183, 203, 204, 209, 213, 216, 221. MARILYN SEGAL: pp. 179, 11, 64 (bottom), 67, 109, 111. MONICA SEGAL: pp. 5, 12, 30, 31, 83, 136, 169, 181. LISA JAFFE: pp. 45, 82, 174, 176, 222. BARRY MICHELSON: pp. 28, 48, 106. PATRICIA LIEBERMAN: pp. 80, 99, 218 STEPHANIE JOFE: pp. 50, 81. DEBBIE FRIEDAN: p. 3. BETTY BARDIGE: p. 33. BETH ST. JOHN: p. 206. NICK MASI: p. 112.

Book design by M.J. DiMassi
Manufactured in the United States of America.

Contents

~~~~~~

~~~~

Foreword

by Samuel J. Meisels, Ph.D.
School of Education, University of Michigan

Marilyn Segal and Betty Bardige have written a marvelous book about the transitions children go through between ages five and eight. This period is a special time in a child's development. After age five children's thought processes are enhanced by the growth of reason, symbolic and abstract thinking, and skills of planning, inference, and complex problem solving. Additional shifts between five and eight years include a newfound ability to focus on more than one dimension of a situation at a time, and an increased use of language to represent one's thoughts and feelings. During this age span, children become increasingly capable of assessing their own skills and performance and are beginning to become more self-reflective.

Children between five and eight years also experience significant social and emotional change. For example, younger children are typically fearful of things that are not directly connected to reality or experience, such as ghosts and monsters. Later, this fear becomes connected to embarrassing one's self or hurting one's self. During this shift, children begin to incorporate other people's observations when formulating their own self-perceptions. Furthermore, children develop greater self-understanding during this time.

This period is not only a time when children experience profound internal development in a variety of domains; it is a time when the world all around them is changing as well. Beginning in kindergarten children go through a wide variety of environmental changes as they make the transition to school. This transition takes place over several years. Children in the early elementary grades experience new peer groups, an increased student-teacher ratio, larger class sizes, a school climate that increasingly compares the abilities of children, new social demands, alterations in family interactions, an increase in structured activities at school, and inter-actions with an increasing number of school personnel.

All children do not experience the five-to-eight-year shift in the same way at the same time. There are individual differences that exist within this period that have important and far-reaching implications for future suc-cess in school.

What Mickey Segal and Betty Bardige have done is to grant us all the rare opportunity of paying a visit to the world of five-to-eight-year-olds in the company of two very remarkable tour guides. This period of dramatic change in the life of the child could not have found better interpreters or more sensitive observers.

The book is clear, comprehensive, and uncompromising. Children aged five to eight are in the midst of an extraordinary period of discovery and questioning. This book does not shy away from any of the topics about which five-to-eight-year-olds are asking, whether the topic is sex, Santa Claus, heaven, the tooth fairy, birth, death, friendships, sibling rivalry, telling jokes and stories, competitive sports, different types of play, or homework assignments. Moreover, Segal and Bardige do not take a distant view of children's lives. Rather, they share the perceptions and experiences of a wide range of children whose stories they weave throughout the vari-ous chapters of the book. Also invaluable are the questions and answers that are included with every chapter. These sections provide wise advice that has obviously been collected over time and from extensive experience. What is so powerful about this, however, is that this advice is not your typ-ical "expert" advice that seems right but is too difficult for real-life parents with real-life problems to put to use. This is practical advice, given it seems, from the inside. It, like the book as a whole, is realistic, clear, direct, and eminently useful.

Read this book and you will know more today than you ever did be-fore about this remarkable, complex, and pivotal period in children's lives. Here you will get answers to questions, a sense of what other children and families besides your own are going through, and great ideas about what you can do to enhance your child's development. But most of all, read this book and enjoy your children!

Introduction

〜〜〜〜〜〜〜〜〜〜〜〜〜〜〜〜〜〜〜〜〜〜〜〜

Your Child at Play: Five to Eight Years, features over thirty families from different parts of the country with one or more children between five and eight years old. We interviewed parents and children, observed and joined children at play at home and at school, collected children's drawings and stories, and held roundtable discussions with primary grade teachers. As we gathered information, we were impressed both by the range of differences among same-age children and by the age-related commonalities that make five to eight a distinct and exciting age group.

The book is divided into eight chapters, describing the different types of play activities that children engage in as they explore ideas, interact with friends and family members, and entertain and teach themselves. Each chapter ends with a question-and-answer section and a collection of play ideas. The questions were offered by parents we interviewed, who shared their concerns and curiosity about their children's play and development. Many of the play ideas were also suggested by parents who had used them successfully with their children.

As we listened to parents' stories, we became more and more excited about the tremendous strides that take place in the five-to-eight-year-old period. Children are playing with new ideas, asking challenging questions, investigating and experimenting, and practicing new skills. They love to gather information and strive to be competent in school as well as in play. They enjoy a wide variety of play activities: active play, pretending, putting on performances, building, creating, and playing games with their friends. Their sense of humor is blossoming and they love jokes and spoofs. They show empathy and concern for others—not only for parents, siblings, and friends, but also for people that they read or hear about. They feel as if everything in the world should be fair and are likely to be outraged if someone is treated unfairly. They continue to feel close to their families, and their parents are likely to be their favorite companions.

We were also intrigued with parents' creativity. Different parents found a myriad of ways to support their children's friendships, encourage their questioning and special interests, and help them maintain their creative spontaneity as they learned to do things in conventional or "correct" ways. Most of all, we were struck by how much parents were enjoying their five-to-eight-year-old children.

Most of the stories we report come from direct observation or were told to us by parents. However, in some cases we have combined similar events or similarly behaving children to create composites that are typical but fictitious. We have changed the names of the children to protect their privacy, except in a few cases where children and their parents asked that we use real names.

This book results from the collaboration of three generations. As mother and daughter, we shared the research and wrote the text together. Other daughters and sons have joined in, contributing observations of their children, as well as questions and suggestions. Most important, the grandchildren have served as sources, inspiration, contributors, and guides.

Writing about five-to-eight-year-olds has been an exciting adventure. We are grateful to the children, parents, and teachers who made this journey possible.

Individual Differences and Common Threads

When I was One,
I had just begun.

When I was Two,
I was nearly new.

When I was Three,
I was hardly Me.

When I was Four,
I was not much more.

When I was Five,
I was just alive.

But now I am Six, I'm as clever as clever.
So I think I'll be six now for ever and ever.

—A. A. MILNE

The five-to-eight-year-old period is a special and exciting time. It is the end of early childhood, a time of fresh discoveries, rich imagination, and special closeness to family. It is also the beginning of school age, a time when children venture out into the world and make new friends, master new skills, and "come into their own" as unique individuals.

We begin this book, and this chapter, by introducing you to some very special children. Each of these children showed special gifts or preoccupations that seemed to be characteristic of them. These strengths shone through when we observed them at play, talked to them about their ideas, listened to their parents' descriptions of their questions, favorite play themes, and relationships, and looked at their creative products. Each of these children is unique, but each is also typical. Their ways of playing and learning, their outlooks on the world, and the activities they enjoyed with family and friends were shared by many of the five-to-eight-year-olds whose families we interviewed.

In this chapter we will look first at individual differences and then at emerging insights that are characteristic of five-to-eight-year-olds in general.

INDIVIDUAL DIFFERENCES

One of the most delightful things about five-to-eight-year-olds is that they are individuals, with distinct personalities and interests of their own. "He's not at all like his older brother," says Ned's mother when asked to describe her seven-year-old son. "He's always thinking about other people. If someone gives Jeffrey a compliment, Ned will report it. Jeffrey would never do that for him."

"My girls have really been good for each other," says Sonia and Marissa's mom, "because they are so different. Marissa's always been physical; if she's not engaged in some kind of gymnastics or athletics, she's climbing the walls—literally. She started competitive gymnastics at five and still loves it; she just has to have an outlet for her physical energy. Sonia has an imagination that fills the world. Now that she's six, she can hook Marissa into her imaginative world. Marissa's even starting to get 'invisible' friends, now that Sonia's introduced her to the idea. And Sonia has learned some physical tricks, like how to ride a bike, from her big sister."

Justin's energy and exuberance are apparent as soon as you meet him. "I can ride a two-wheeler. I am just learning to

ride a skateboard. I went down the driveway and jumped." "You won't believe it! I'm the first one in the family to figure out the new TV controls." "Sometimes I can use magic. I can make cars stop sometimes. I used my magic to be Star of the Week."

The superhero of his own fantasies, Justin is forever engaged in battle. As he plays, he scoops up toys, objects, people, phrases, and ideas—whatever is at hand becomes part of his imaginative world. He'll kill you with his light saber, then zap you instantly back to life. He can run at "light speed," or at least "hyperspeed," "as fast as a Komodo dragon, and they're really, really fast."

Ask Justin about his friends, and he'll tell you about the club he organized, with "officers and normal people," and how they fought the "bug people." Ask about his favorite computer games, and he'll tell you his favorites are "games where you go out and conquer planets and destroy aliens and as you get 'gooder' you discover nuclear power and laser guns and electric things." Justin's parents sometimes worry about his preoccupation with war games, but mostly they realize that Justin is just playing, and real violence is anathema to him. Even Justin's drawings reveal his playful intent: His picture of a fight in which the little guy loses shows a smiling little guy who looks more as if he's holding hands with the big guy than as if he's punching or warding off blows.

Caroline, like Justin, is a storyteller, but her style is very different. If she didn't enjoy it so much, you might call her a workaholic. She's always busy, writing books, making lists of things to do, playing school with her dolls, practicing the piano,

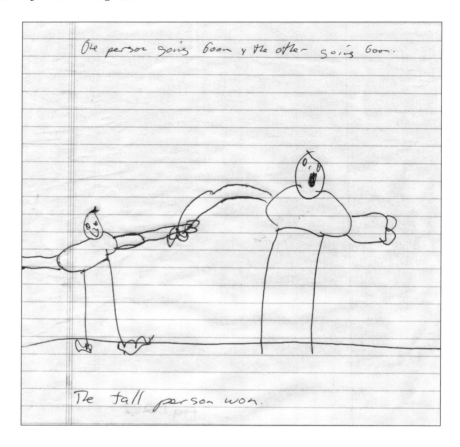

reading books or watching videos to get ideas for her stories. As her third-grade class studies Native Americans, Caroline writes a book about a Native American child who loses her family and has to survive on her own until they can find her. This is one of "a billion" that she says she is working on right now.

Though Caroline writes in a wide range of genres, most of her books contain some humor. One of her first, "The Hat in the Hat," is a modern version of *The 500 Hats of Bartholomew Cubbins*, complete with TV coverage for Harry, the hero. A poem about a bad dream reveals both her delight in wordplay and her use of the written word to express and master uncomfortable feelings.

I had bad dreams two nights in a row.
One was real scary, the other I don't know!
One made me scream, the other—it's a mystery!
When I stop thinking about them,
My bad dreams will be history!
I hope my terrible thoughts will go soon,
If they don't, my face will turn maroon!
I shall sue the author of my terrible dreams,
Then he'll be up to no nasty schemes!
Soon I'll have freedom, I'll live in great peace,
I'll run around like a gaggle of geese!
Today is the day I will prove that man wrong,
I don't think he'll last very long!

A friendly child with strong opinions, Caroline is sometimes the "odd one out," both at school and at home. When the girls in her class chat about "boys, clothes, dancing, and acting cool" or her brothers spend hours watching sports on TV, Caroline finds other pursuits. Yet Caroline is able to use her writing to make social connections. Most of her stories are good enough that other children enjoy them; Caroline sometimes gives them as presents to special friends, and frequently shares them at school. She was thrilled when her teacher used one of the stories she had shared as the basis of a class assignment.

Xavier, like Caroline, is aware that he's different from his peers. He, too, is a "brain," full of questions and speculations on a wide range of subjects. He wants to know what is beyond the universe, and whether God would still exist if the solar system were sucked into a black hole. He noticed that water feels heavier when he puts his hand right under the faucet, and wonders what force is at work. He believes in reincarnation, and wonders who he might have been before he was Xavier and what he might someday remember from his former life. He notices differences in skin colors, beliefs, languages, and traditions, and wants to know their sources. "Why are people different colors?" "Why do Christians celebrate Christmas?" "Who was Jesus; what was his life like; why do people believe in him?" Fluent in both Spanish and English, Xavier was bored

with the required Spanish class at his school. His solution was to invent three different versions of "Spanish Pig Latin."

Like other boys his age, Xavier likes to dress up as an action hero or a magician and put on a show for his family. He enjoys soccer, bike riding, and swimming; likes board games and Nintendo; readily joins a group but especially enjoys being with his best friend. But Xavier also has interests that fewer of his peers share: he likes to read books in Spanish as well as English; he enjoys playing chess and doing math problems; he loves puzzles.

Xavier doesn't like being different. He winces when boys and girls tease him for being a "brain." And he often lets himself be manipulated, both by his best friend and by the more casual groups he joins, preferring not to stand out too much or resist the social flow.

Kate is also full of questions, but hers are more practical than Xavier's. "How does Santa get down the chimney?" "Why do people smoke?" "Why won't Daddy lose weight like the doctor says he should?" "Does God get hungry?" Kate worries and wonders about children whose parents are divorced, gets upset when someone else's feelings are hurt, and would rather lose a game that everyone thought was fun than win one and have a friend be angry or upset. She likes going fishing with her father, but has to make sure that the fish aren't hurt when she throws them back. She loves helping in the aviary at school, and wishes she could have a fish, a prairie dog, and a woodchuck for pets. Though she kills mosquitoes without compunction, she carefully carried a roach out of the house and placed it gently in the grass.

Kate likes to read to her family. Her drawings are full of rainbows, stars, hearts, and happy-looking faces. She hates violence on TV, and insists that it be turned off. The stories she tells have morals and happy endings. She likes to put on her

best dress for dinner, and to accompany her parents wherever they go. Her parents describe her as sweet and compassionate, and note that she plays easily and happily with other children, whether they are her age, younger, or older. She is also quite good at entertaining herself.

Kate has two best friends, Katie and Kaitlin. Katie is much like Kate, sunny and sometimes silly, more concerned with playing than winning, and eager to play a nurturant role. Kaitlin is more brash and competitive, more likely to say things that adults disapprove of, sometimes even possessive and demanding. She's also a lot of fun to play with because she thinks of things to do that Kate would not come up with on her own. Playing with Kaitlin gives Kate an opportunity to try out different behaviors and expand her repertoire. Kate's mother isn't always thrilled with Kate's "personality change," especially when Kate picks up swear words, smart-alecky rejoinders, and story lines from movies that she won't let Kate see. At the same time, she recognizes how much Kate enjoys the relationship, and continues to arrange opportunities for the girls to get together.

Steven combines Kate's tenderheartedness with Xavier's scientific curiosity, Justin's thirst for adventure, and Caroline's competent creativity. His mother describes him as the "sweetest, kindest, gentlest, most loving, most empathetic child you would ever want to know." Steven was chosen by his school to be a companion to Andrew, a four-year-old with autism. When his mother asked him if he liked playing with

Andrew, he replied with enthusiasm, "Andrew and I have lots of fun together. He doesn't really have a problem. It's just that he doesn't understand the rules."

Steven has a warm and loving relationship with both his mother and his father. He and his mother cook together, finish furniture, and do magic tricks. Recognizing his fascination with how things work, his mother takes him to the science museum on a regular basis. These visits inevitably inspire Steven's creative inventions—like his multipurpose utensils, his traps for invisible barges, and the miniature golf obstacle course that he created out of boxes and cartons. When Steven is with his father they share their interest in alternative music. Father and son take turns pretending to be the DJ as they play their favorite tapes.

Steven's gentleness is evident in his interactions with his family, in his pretend play, and in his expression of fears. When his big sister, Jenna, needles him or becomes physical, Steven's response is verbal. "Jenna, you know we are not supposed to hurt each other. If you don't stop right away I am going to have to put you in time-out."

Steven's play themes typically revolve around adventure. He loves to set up campsites in his room, gathering up cushions, blankets, books, Alfred, his huggy bear, corn chips, and a flashlight. Every five minutes or so Steven picks up his flashlight and makes a quick foray out of his campsite. When he returns to his tent he hugs Alfred, assuring him that the wolves, bears, and wildcats have gone somewhere else.

While Steven plays the role of Alfred's protector, he steers away from confrontation, even when the dangers that lurk around him are figments of his imagination. "Are you sure there are no monsters in this house?" Steven asked his mother.

When she assured him that there were not, Steven responded, "Well, I'm still scared anyway. You can never quite tell with monsters. They are very tricky. They can come in a split second, and you wouldn't even know it."

As evidenced by his rich imagination, Steven is an unusually creative as well as gentle child. He devises all kinds of magic tricks, talks to his mother in a secret language that he invented, creates interesting, if not always palatable recipes, and makes up original jokes. "Why did the pitcher hit the ball? Because he was not the catcher."

The most compelling evidence of Steven's creativity are the freehand drawings he makes. His drawings are not only beautifully executed, but each tells an original story. One drawing features a pitched tent, with several playful goblins dancing around it. Another depicts an astronaut loaded with gear stepping into a space capsule. A particularly interesting drawing by Steven demonstrates both his creativity and his gentleness. It shows a row of soldiers, beating their drums, walking through a field of flowers.

COMMON THREADS

Despite the wide range of individual differences among children five to eight, there are also striking commonalities. The most dramatic are the emerging insights and convictions that permeate the conversations of children in this age group.

Distinguishing between Real and Pretend

One of the delightful characteristics of children between five and eight years old is their ability to believe that something is true, while knowing at the same time it is not true. Children can recognize Santa Claus couldn't possibly come down everyone's chimney in the same night but continue to believe that

Santa Claus exists. Children may be able to state quite clearly that a doll is just pretend and at the same time act as if the doll is real.

Katie was playing dolls with her cousin. When it was time for her to come home, Katie took her doll, Samantha, into the car. "Caroline and I were pretending to take Samantha and Molly on a picnic." "That must have been fun," her mother remarked, "but now we have to get home. Jump into the car." "Okay," Katie responded, "but wait a minute. Samantha forgot to say good-bye to Molly."

Katie's confusion about real and pretend became obvious one day when she was watching TV. While watching *E.R.* with her mother, she had stated quite matter-of-factly that the blood wasn't real; it was just ketchup. However, when a Disney film came on, Katie refused to watch. The death of Bambi's mother and the Lion King's father had traumatized her, and she was not going to take a chance watching a Disney movie in which another terrible thing might happen.

The difficulty in distinguishing between real and pretend is often reflected in a child's fears. Steven was convinced that there were monsters in the house, and his mother could not convince him that there were not. "But Mom," he explained, "you would not really know if the monsters came into the house. They could come in one split second, and you may not even see them."

The five-to-seven-year-old is intrigued by magicians and considers books or movies with magical themes, such as fairy tales or Disney films, as fully credible. By eight years old children are still intrigued with magic tricks, and especially interested in doing magic tricks themselves. They try to make a distinction between what is real magic and what is trick magic, but are not likely to question the reality of "real" magic.

Between five and eight years old, children are beginning to recognize that there may be a difference between what appears to be a fact and what is really a fact. They are fascinated with magic mirrors that distort the way you look, colored paddles that make objects different colors, or microscopes that make small objects appear to be big. Although young children are able to realize that appearances may not reflect reality, they also put stock in what they see or hear, and are often surprised when there is a mismatch between how something seems to be and how something really is.

James was in the bathtub playing with the clear plastic top of a bottle. "That's funny," he said to his mother. "The top is

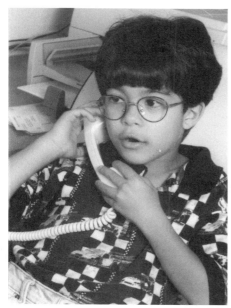

really wet, but it looks as if it is dry." In contrast to James, Benjamin had difficulty separating appearances and reality. When his great grandmother was very ill, she did not put on her dentures. "Was your grandmother mean?" he asked his mother. "No? Well, she looked mean."

Just as children are struggling to separate appearance from reality, they may also have difficulty distinguishing between what is true and what is just teasing. Xavier was told by his friend John that his father was a pirate. Xavier wasn't convinced that his friend John was telling the truth, but he felt compelled to investigate. He called John's father and left a message on his answering machine. "John told me that you were a pirate, but I don't think it's true. Please call back."

Black-and-White Thinking

According to most children in the five-to-eight age range, the world is black or white, with no shades in between. If you are not following the letter of the law, you are bad. If you do something bad, you should go to jail; and if you don't understand, you are stupid. "Do robbers have friends?" Justin asked his family. His big brother's explanation, "Sure, other robbers and people they grew up with," was unsatisfying. Robbers were outside the law, and therefore should be exiled from the social world.

Fahran learned in religious school that there were good deeds and bad deeds. Doing good deeds will get you into heaven. He also learned that children should listen to sacred music rather than modern music. One day he caught his sister listening to pop music on the radio. He hurried downstairs to his mother. "My sister is doing a bad deed," he reported, concerned that she would be barred from heaven forever.

Alex drove his bicycle up to the corner playground and discovered beer cans and cigarette butts under one of the structures. "There were bad boys here," he told his mother. "You better call the police."

An interesting facet of black-and-white thinking is a firm belief in facts. Grade school children become enamored with facts and will not accept a distortion, even if it is only in fun. Ethan told his mother that the Barney show was bad for kids because it teaches incorrect facts. "Barney sang a song that says Sally the camel has five humps."

Taking Things Too Literally

Katie, at age six, was visiting a bunny farm with her mother. She learned that you had to touch the mother bunny to get her scent before you petted the baby bunnies. As long as the mother recognized her own scent on her babies, she would take them back. Katie followed the directions carefully and had fun petting the bunnies. After a while her mother called her. "It's time to have lunch now, Katie. Give the baby bunny back to her mother and then wash your hands." Katie dutifully washed her hands and then went back and patted the mother bunny. "Katie, what are you doing?" her mother asked. "I have to give the mother bunny back her scent," Katie explained. For Katie, the scent was a thing that she had borrowed from the mother bunny and had to return.

Angela held a similarly literal concept of God. Discussing Princess Diana's death with her mother, Angela had trouble accepting the fact that Diana had died so young. Attempting to comfort her, her mother explained, "It was her time." "When is it someone's time?" asked Angela. "Only God knows," replied her mother. "Oh," responded Angela, "can you ask him?"

Kevin had been given a Native American dream catcher to hang in his window where it could catch the bad dreams and let only the good ones through. Several weeks later, Kevin complained, "Mommy, my dream catcher isn't working. I had a really bad nightmare last night. Can you get me some sage smoke so I can clean it properly?"

Endre, whose family attends church each Sunday, took his classmates' wedding vows literally.

Endre: Mother, did you know that Janet and Matthew are married?

Mother: You mean they are pretending to be married. You can't get married when you are six years old.

Endre: No, honest, Mommy, they're married. They had a wedding in the school play.

In other incidents, children's misinterpretations hinged on partial understanding of words, as well as a tendency to overgeneralize or to interpret words too literally.

Crystal and her father were buying some bananas at a fruit stand. Her father opened his wallet and discovered that all he had was a one-hundred-dollar bill. "I guess I'll have to break the bill," he told his daughter. "It's the only thing I have." His daughter was horrified. "Daddy, no, you're not supposed to break a bill."

Ned had heard on television that sports star Larry Bird

had retired. Ned's baby-sitter brought her father over to meet Ned. "I brought my dad here because he retired," she explained to Ned. Ned looked at the baby-sitter's father. "Oh, are you Larry Bird?" he asked.

Stories like these often become treasured family in-jokes. Ned's extended family had a special name for his unintentionally funny literalisms—"the world according to Ned."

When adult descriptions are vague, literal-minded children often invent their own more specific images. Benjamin was very upset when his grandmother died. "I'm real angry with God," he told his father. "Give me a ladder and some rope. I'm going to make a rope ladder and climb up and get her. God's keeping her there against her will."

Katie's picture of Heaven was even more elaborate. When Katie's dog died, her mother tried to comfort her. "Gilda went up to heaven to be with Jennifer," she explained to Katie. "No, Mommy, you got it all wrong. There are two heavens, one heaven is the Jesus heaven and you have to stay there for a while. Then you go over a bridge and you're in God's heaven where Jennifer is. Gilda will go to Jennifer when it's time."

When Shawn's mother was pregnant with his little brother, Shawn tried to envision what it was like inside the womb. "The baby has a little couch to sit on," he told his mom. "He has a little glass, and when you take a drink of water he holds it up and catches the drips so he can have a drink, too."

Inflexibility of Thinking

Children, in particular children from six to eight years old, can be very set in their ideas. Once they have solidified an idea, they have difficulty changing their thinking, even in the face of contrary evidence. If they have settled on a hypothesis, they will not entertain alternatives.

Katie had decided that hills and mountains are the same

thing. When her nana tried to explain the difference between a hill and a mountain, Katie would not accept her explanation. She told her nana in her most authoritative voice, "Hill is the nickname for mountain."

Recognizing Different Points of View

Although five-to-eight-year-olds often think in black-and-white terms and cling tenaciously to their ideas, at around seven years old they begin to appreciate different points of view. "Daddy thinks that the best place to go hiking is North Carolina and Mommy says West Virginia." The seven-year-old recognizes that both mother and dad can be right according to their own perspective but may have difficulty figuring out why their perspectives differ.

Caroline got into a discussion with her father about whether there was a God. Caroline made it clear that God existed because lots of people said so. Her father was skeptical. "But I don't believe in God because nobody has ever seen him." Caroline shook her head. "You know, Daddy, I can believe whatever I want to believe, and you can believe whatever you want to believe."

Concern with Fairness

"It's not fair" is a constant refrain in the five-to-eight-year-old years. It is not fair if you don't get equal treatment, if somebody cheats in a game, or if someone doesn't give you a turn. It is also not fair if someone else is not treated right. It is not fair if a child doesn't have as much of something as everybody else, if a child is mistreated by his parent, or if a child is deprived of something for no good reason.

When Jessica's sister got a stuffed animal and she didn't, or when her best friend got a dog, Jessica repeated the favorite refrain, "Mommy, it's not fair." But her idea of fairness went beyond wanting equal treatment. She was also upset if someone was treated unfairly, even if it was only in a story.

Jessica was listening to a story in which the main character is unfairly punished for slapping a friend because her friend slapped her and then lied about who did the slapping. Jessica was agitated and insisted that her mother keep reading until the problem was resolved. Jessica seemed to take it personally, as if she had been wronged. She reacted similarly when Anne of Green Gables was falsely accused of theft.

After watching a TV account of Princess Diana's death, Marvin was angry. It wasn't fair that two boys should lose their mother. It wasn't fair that the oldest son in the royal family got to be the king. Kevin had a similar response when he learned about the Middle Passage. "A bunch of people kidnapped other people and put them on a boat and didn't take care of them. That wasn't fair! How can people own other people?"

Steven's sense of fairness extended even to someone who may not have felt cheated. One day Steven went to the grocery store with his mother. On the way out a little boy took a bar of candy off the shelf and proceeded to eat it. His mother said nothing to him as he munched on the candy bar. "Why didn't his mother scold him?" Steven asked. "He's never going to learn how to behave if his mother lets him get away with things. It's not fair."

Following Rules

Children in the five-to-eight-year-old bracket are obsessed with rules. Five-year-olds love the idea of following a rule and are perfectly willing to comply with something if they know it is a rule. Kindergarten teachers find that the best way to keep their classes running smoothly is to let the children help them make a list of classroom rules. Once it's a rule, it's a law, and you can't disobey a law. Six-to-seven-year-olds carry the obsession with rules one step further. They change the rules of a game either to increase their chance of winning or to make a game more fun, or they create the rules for their own invented game. At the same time, they are insistent about their parents following rules. If they see a sign that says "Speed limit 30 miles an hour," they insist that their parents drive thirty miles an hour, no faster and no slower. By eight years old most children are able to read the rules of a game, and are convinced that following the rules makes the game more fair and more fun. But despite this concern with playing by the rules, cheating in a game to make yourself the winner is not out of the question.

Eight-year-old Marissa was upset one day because she "cheated" on a problem-solving assignment at school. Stymied, she looked at another child's paper "to help me get started." The school encourages collaboration, Marissa "understood the concept," and the assignment was not in any sense a test. However, Marissa still felt that she might have done something wrong, and needed her mother's help in drawing the line between getting started and cheating.

Self-Awareness

Between five and eight years old, children become increasingly aware of who they are. They are learning about themselves by constantly comparing themselves with their peers. Am I good in sports? Am I smarter than the other kids? Am I a good artist? Am I the fastest reader, the best writer? Am I the first one in the class to finish my spelling, math, or reading assignment?

Xavier recognized that he was the smartest kid in the class, but he was not always happy about it. He hated being called "brainy" and thought of it as a stigma. In contrast, Endre was worried about not being smart enough. He recognized that he was not placed in a group with the smart kids. "Am I smart?" he kept asking his mother. And no matter how hard his mother tried to assure him, Endre asked the question over and over.

Katie feels good about herself and has no problem comparing herself with other children. "I am a bad artist," she told her mother, "but I really like to draw." Similarly, Danny is quite happy to be the "second fastest runner" in his class.

ANSWERS TO PARENTS' QUESTIONS

I've heard that five to eight is the easiest time with children. Is that true?

Every age for every child generates both challenges and delights. Most children in the five-to-eight age range are attached to their parents, anxious to please, basically trustworthy, and motivated to excel. They are usually easygoing and fun to play with, though they can sometimes be moody, stubborn, or clingy. Their developing physical prowess and desire to venture farther from home faces parents with the challenge of encouraging independence and initiative while keeping their child safe. Another challenge is social skill development. Parents want their children to be accepted by their peers and to develop close, enduring relationships. Children often need parents' help in making friends, arranging play dates, negotiating conflicts, and dealing with hurt feelings. At the same time, children need to learn to do these things on their own.

How much time should five-to-eight-year-olds spend in organized activities outside of school? How can I tell if my child is overscheduled or underscheduled?

There is a fine line between overscheduling and underscheduling children, and parents must draw the line in a way that fits the temperament of their child. Typically, five-to-eight-year-olds do well with one to three outside activities, such as sports, religious school, and music lessons. Overscheduling is usually more of a danger than underscheduling; children need to have enough downtime to play freely with friends, with you, and by themselves. Pretending, daydreaming, and just fooling around are important ways of relaxing, learning, and discovering new interests. However, some very intense children become moody or demanding when they do not have enough challenge or stimulation, or "climb the walls" when they do not get enough structured physical activity. These children often have special talents and interests that emerge early, and do well in intensive programs such as children's theater or gymnastics teams. Take your cues from your child.

Can you trust the age-level recommendations on toys?

In terms of safety, yes. Suggested age spans are also usually appropriate in terms of interest level, but, especially in areas of special skill or interest, you may find that your child enjoys toys recommended for older, or even for younger, children.

My son is very sensitive and expressive. How can I help him maintain these strengths as he gets older, and not have to act "cool" or "tough"?

Children do not lose their sensitivity or expressiveness as they get older, but they may express these characteristics in different ways. It is quite natural for children to feel that they are too big to kiss and hug their parents. It is also natural for children to act "cool" or "tough" so that they are accepted as a part of the peer group. That does not mean that they have lost desirable characteristics; they may express affection with pats, special handshakes, or in-jokes and show their sensitivity to others by being quietly helpful or suggesting appropriate play ideas.

Some boys do feel pressured to develop a more "macho" image, or are teased when they do not. One thing you can do is to encourage your son's school to adopt programs that encourage empathy, cooperation, and positive ways of resolving conflicts. These programs give children permission to express their feelings, and help develop their nurturant and expressive skills. You can also provide your son with opportunities to play with a variety of friends, including younger and older children, girls, friends from early childhood, and friends who share his creative interests. If your son is uncomfortable with things his more macho friends enjoy, you can give him rules that he can blame on you. "My dad won't let me watch that kind of movie." "My mom lets me play sports video games, but I'm not ever allowed to watch the fighting games." If your son is teased for being interested in "girl" activities, a matter-of-fact explanation is usually his best response. "I'm not a sissy. I just think ballet is fun. Want me to teach you some leaps?"

My son wants to be cool like the other kids. He is always asking me to buy him the latest fad—oversized shirts; long, wide-legged pants; and to make matters worse he wants to wear this stuff at the most inappropriate times. Any suggestions?

Although there are no hard and fast rules about dress, the time to make a compromise is when you buy the clothes. "Yes, I will buy you wide-legged jeans but you can only wear them when you play."

PLAY IDEAS

- Keep a record of your child's questions, funny comments, and original ideas. You will enjoy looking back on it together.
- Provide special spaces where your child can pursue her unique interests. An unused corner of a basement or garage can be turned into a "studio" for a budding artist or a "workbench" for a child who likes to make "inventions" out of scrap materials. A budding writer might appreciate an office; an athlete might help create a storage area for sports equipment, with display space for trophies and sports cards.
- Create a file or portfolio in which you can keep your child's artwork, writing, and best schoolwork.
- Give your child a bulletin board to decorate with items that reflect her interests or with her own pictures, lists, and writings.

- Give your child a "treasure box" for special items.
- Create a "Me Book" with your child that highlights her unique characteristics and interests. You can use a commercial version, such as *My Book About Me*, by Dr. Seuss, or make up your own framework. You might include things like: my name and how I got it, my nicknames, who is in my family, things I like to do, things I hate, things I am good at, things I like to learn about, my favorite places, foods I like and hate, my best friends, my collections, my wishes, when I grow up. Children can illustrate these books with drawings, stickers, or photographs.
- Capitalize on your child's emerging understanding of time by posting a large family calendar. Help your child mark his special events and plans with pictures or stickers and count the days till the big event.
- Capitalize on your child's emerging interest in "adult" conversations and issues by allowing her to contribute to the conversation. Even when you can't take her suggestions or agree with her explanation, let her know that her ideas are interesting and helpful. Look for books, videos, and outings that provide opportunities to discuss similar ideas and issues.
- Capitalize on your child's interest in rules by playing board games, strategy games, word games, and active games. Seek out some cooperative board games, where everyone works together to win. In competitive games, encourage your child to help you modify rules and scoring systems so that everyone has a "fair" chance to win.
- Encourage your child to teach you games she learns at school or that she invents.
- Capitalize on your child's continuing interest in fantasy, magic, and pretending by going along with his pretenses. Follow his lead in treating stuffed animals as family members, monster-proofing his bedroom, or interacting with

his superhero self. Introduce fantasies yourself on occasion: Leave a note from the tooth fairy or Santa Claus; talk to a new doll, stuffed animal, or action figure as if it is an old friend; tell stories about the elves and fairies that live in the grass or the animal families hiding in the trees; choose read-aloud books with fantasy themes.

• Teach your child some magic tricks or card tricks. Here is a simple card trick: Ask a friend to pick a card, look at it, and put it back in the deck. Deal out the whole deck, face up, in six rows of nine cards each (the last row will only have seven cards). Ask your friend to point out the row that her card is in. Pick up that row; then pick up the rest of the cards, keeping the first row on top. Deal the cards out face up again, but this time deal by columns. Put nine cards in the first column, then nine in the second, etc. The

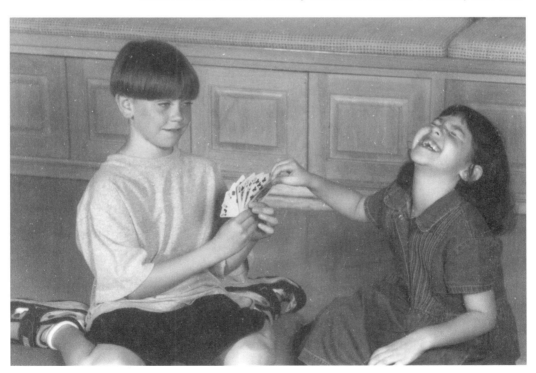

last column will only have seven cards. Again, ask the friend to point out which row his card is in. It will be the first card in that row. If you wish, you can deal out the cards again before identifying the card.

- Keep a photo album of the special events in your child's life. If he would like to, your child can take part in labeling the photos.

CHAPTER 2

The Questions Children Ask

How can I go to sleep at night?
How can I go to bed?
With oh so many puzzling things,
Racing around in my head.

Today turns into yesterday,
And here turns into there.
Tomorrow never comes at all.
I do not think it's fair!

Because they are noticing, learning, and putting together so many things, five-to-eight-year-olds are full of questions. The "why's" of the three-and-four-year-olds gradually give way to the demands for detailed explanations and the "I think this is true but I'm not sure" formulations of the early-school-ager.

In this chapter we examine children's questions about the physical world, the natural world, the social world, and the supernatural world. These questions tell us not only what children want to know but how they are conceptualizing their world.

THE PHYSICAL WORLD

The questions that five-to-eight-year-old children ask about the physical world reflect a new level of thinking. They ask abstract questions about time, space, and distance and sometimes come

up with questions that parents have difficulty with. These questions demonstrate an emerging ability to think in abstractions. They may also reveal misconceptions that children have about their physical world.

Time

For preschool children, time is associated with past or upcoming events. The ability to conceptualize historical time, even when their ideas are inaccurate or confused, is a significant advance.

Kevin, who loved to read fact books, asked his mother, "If infinity goes on forever, what numbers come after infinity?" Becky's question was not quite as sophisticated. "I know that some people lived a long time ago—but when did time get started?" Katie had a conversation with her mother that revealed both an interest in a long time ago and a confusion with what "long ago" meant. Her brother Kenneth, a freshman in college, was enrolled in an integrated program that focused on ancient Greece. Katie accompanied her parents on a visiting weekend and listened intently to their talk about ancient Greek studies. Finally, she posed the question, "What does ancient Greece mean?" Her mother worked hard formulating an answer. "Greece," she explained, "is a country far away on the other side of the ocean. When we talk about ancient Greece, we talk about what Greece was like over a thousand years ago." "Were there mountain goats in ancient Greece?" Katie asked. "I am not sure," her mother answered, feeling certain now that Katie understood the concept of ancient. Katie asked a third question that burst her mother's bubble. "Mother, a thousand years ago when Greece was ancient, did you read books about it?"

Even when children understand the concept of "a long time ago," it takes a while for them to put events from the distant past into any sort of order. Darryl asked, "Did Jesus come before the dinosaurs?"

Other questions about time reflect an attempt to understand its measurement. "Why does my birthday come on different days each year?" "When I turn six on my birthday, will I be a different age than my friends?" "How come some months have more days than others?" "Why is Christmas always on December 25th, and Chanukah keeps moving around?" Children also begin to recognize that the time can be different in different places. Alan, whose grandparents live in a faraway time zone, was curious about time at the North Pole. "What time is it where Santa is?" Megan found a newspaper article explaining when an eclipse could be watched in different parts of the country. She read the times out loud until she came to noon. "Mommy," she asked, "what sort of time is noon?"

Space

With all the talk about space exploration and the showing of movies like *Star Wars,* it is not at all surprising that children are interested in what is happening outside of the earth. As with the concept of time, children have difficulty understanding that space keeps going on and their questions reveal their puzzlement. Xavier, who was always posing difficult questions, asked his mother, "What is there beyond the universe?" "What will happen if the earth and the solar system are sucked into a black hole? Will there still be a God?" Becky lacked Xavier's sophisticated vocabulary but asked the same kind of questions. "Dad, tell me, where does the sky end?" Fortunately, most questions that children ask about space are not as hard to answer as Xavier's and Becky's questions. Several children asked ques-

tions about the moon, the planets, and the stars. "Why are there more stars in Ocala than there are in Fort Lauderdale?" "Why does the moon come out in the daytime when it's supposed to come out at night?" "How can you tell if you're looking at a star or a planet?" "Where does the sun go when it isn't out anymore?" "Why does the moon sometimes look like a ball and sometimes look like a slice of cheese?"

Geography

Casey was looking at a map of North America that showed the states and provinces. After staring at the map for several minutes, Casey asked his teacher, "How come all the states and provinces fit so well together?" At first his teacher was perplexed. Finally, she realized that Casey was thinking of the map as a puzzle. He could not differentiate between border lines and topological features. Like Casey, Kate was unable to distinguish between countries and topology. She went fishing with her dad on an island just south of Key West. "Dad, when are we going back to Florida?"

Alice, who was just turning five, had difficulty understanding distance. She was watching a History Channel show with her parents that was about India. "What's India?" Alice asked. "It's a country far away," her father answered, "on the other side of the world." "But how far is it to India?" Alice continued. "What is it like there? Can we walk there?"

Weather

Weather is a frequent topic of conversation in many children's homes. Some of their questions relate to everyday experiences. Other questions relate to less frequent and more scary phenomena.

Rain, snow, wind, and tides are common weather conditions that are likely to prompt questions. The more Kevin learned about rain, the more questions he had. "What makes rain? How does the water get up in the sky? What's evaporation? Why does it come down? Where does it go? What does the ground do with it?" It just didn't make sense that rain could disappear into the ground and then somehow get back up into the sky. Justin was also puzzled by the explanations about rain he had received. When a friend of Justin's mother asked him what makes rain, he tried to answer. "Clouds, when they get heavy." The friend asked how that worked. "I'm only guessing this," he answered. "Is it that the sun evaporates the water and it gets into the clouds and gets stuck?"

Kate, who loves to jump waves when she goes to the beach, is puzzled by the phenomenon. "What makes the ocean wave?" She also wants to know, "What causes lightning?" James, who lives in Florida, had his first experience with snow when his family traveled to Colorado. "Why is snow so cold?"

"Does snow come out of the clouds?" "What's the difference between a snow cloud and a rain cloud?" "Why is the wind so cold?" "Where did it come from and where is it going?"

By far, the most frequent questions about weather have to do with dangerous conditions. Angela went to visit Colombia with her parents. She had helped her parents collect blankets that they had sent to earthquake victims in Colombia a year before their trip. As soon as they got to Colombia, Angela asked if there was going to be an earthquake. Probably not, her mother replied. Angela continued with her questions: "How do you know when an earthquake is coming?" Her mother answered truthfully: "You really can't tell." Angela asked only one more question: "Why don't we just go home?"

Tornadoes, like earthquakes, were a source of concern for many children. Mark asked his grandfather, "What do the clouds look like when there is going to be a tornado? Are they darker than the sky, darker than the night? I know they are darker than the sun."

Steven saw photos of a tornado on television and was quite concerned. "What is a tornado?" he asked. As soon as his mother began to explain, he put up his hands. "Stop, Mom, don't tell me anymore, I'm only a kid!"

What Things Are Made Of

"What is this rock made of?" asks Crystal, a budding geologist who loves to collect and identify rocks. "Are white rocks made from the same stuff as black ones?" "How come this one is smooth and this one is rough?" "Are they made of the same stuff?" "Why are some rocks big and some rocks little?" "Are little rocks made of the same stuff as big ones?" "What about sand? Why is it so many different colors?" "Is brown sand made from brown rocks?" Crystal, like many other children her age, is trying to figure out which of the differences she sees are associated with substance, and which are associated merely with form.

"Why is the sky blue?" asks Becky. "And what are clouds made of?" "Why do they have to mix cement? How do they make the bricks?" asks Christopher as he watches workers lay a walk. "What is the lava made from?" Brittany asks when she learns about volcanoes on a trip to Hawaii. "If snow is frozen water," asks Justin, "how come it's white?" Xavier's questions send his parents scrambling for reference books. "What is the Eiffel Tower made of?" "What is coal made of and why is it a source of energy?" "Are there atoms and molecules in light?"

How Things Work

From the time they are infants, children are curious about how things work. This curiosity continues unabated with children five to eight years old, and the questions may continue nonstop.

"Why do cars need gas?" "How does the toilet work?" "Why does the water feel heavier when you put your hand right under the faucet?" "Why does steam come out of the manholes?" "How can airplanes write in the sky?"

Electricity is particularly puzzling to children and is the source of many questions. Dana had a long conversation with her mother. "Do power lines go all over the entire world?" "Yes." "Even in the jungle?" "No." "Then what do they use for power?" "Candles." "How do they make candles in the jungle?" "I don't know." "Mom, kids need to know this stuff."

THE NATURAL WORLD

Plants and Animals

Expectedly, many of the questions that children ask are related to the natural world. Putting together what they observe with what they learn from books and from older people, children ask questions about plants and animals that often take adults by

THE QUESTIONS CHILDREN ASK   37

surprise. "Why does a dog have a tail and I don't?" "Were squash, string beans, and apples once alive? Yes? Well, then, what kind of animal did they come from?" "How do ducks swim? What keeps them up on top of the water?" "What keeps birds up in the air?" "Where do cows sleep at night?" "Do vampire bats suck blood?" "Why does a dog's tongue hang out of its mouth?" "A spider is not an insect because it has eight legs. Would it become an insect if you pulled off two of its legs?"

Sometimes by identifying with animals and sometimes by watching them, children notice things that are not described in their books. As with other natural phenomena, their questions reflect their attempt to meld what they have learned from different sources into a coherent whole.

Dinosaurs

Most young children are intrigued by dinosaurs. Although their interest in dinosaurs is fueled by movies like *Jurassic Park*, the fascination with dinosaurs is more likely to be related to the fantastic characteristics of dinosaurs. "How big is a dinosaur?" "Where do dinosaurs come from?" "Were dinosaurs on earth before I was?" "Were there dinosaurs all over the earth?" "Which dinosaurs like to eat meat?" "Why do some dinosaurs like green stuff?" "Where did dinosaurs choose to lay their eggs?" "Mommy, is it true? Dinosaurs were real a long time ago but now they are only fiction?"

Some children, like Ethan, become dinosaur experts, able to identify twenty or thirty different kinds and to recognize subtle distinctions, such as the tendency of toy companies to mislabel a three-toed allosaur as T-Rex, which has only two fingers on its hands. Others, like Arran, become fascinated with the idea of extinction, and may even concoct their own theories to explain the dinosaurs' demise. "Maybe they ate poison plants and got sick and then when the asteroid hit the earth and made the sky all dark they got cold and died." Angela's worry is also typical. "Is an asteroid going to happen again and then will we die?"

The Human Body

Some of the questions children ask are about the human body, how it is made, and how it works. "What do kidneys do?" "Why do cuts bleed?" "Why don't girls have a penis?" "How come people call poop dirty? All it is is food that goes into your mouth and comes out the other end."

Other questions children ask have to do with growth and how the body changes. "What makes my body grow?" "When will I grow boobs?" " Will I have to wear a bra?" "Is hair going to grow on my legs?" "When will I have to shave?"

Other questions reflect an attempt to understand the "stay-healthy messages" given by parents and the media. "Is fat bad for you?" "Mommy, did you smoke or drink while you were pregnant?" "Is sugar-free gum good for you?" "Do hash brown potatoes count as healthy food?"

Birth and Death

Perhaps because they are mysterious, but very close to home, all five-to-eight-year-olds ask questions about birth and death. These questions escalate when children experience the birth of a baby or the death of someone close to them. Inevitably as children seek to understand birth, they question their own origins. Children also tend to personalize death. They recognize that someday they will die and so will their parents.

Birth

The most asked questions about birth are how a baby is made, and how does it come out of "Mommy's tummy." Christopher, who watched a TV show about the birth of a baby, expressed

his amazement: "Is that how a baby is made? Is that how I came out?" When children recognize that a baby grows inside their mommy's "tummy" and then comes out, they are likely to start worrying. "Does it hurt to have a baby?" "Will it be bloody?" "Do I have to have a baby?" "How does a baby get out of his mommy's tummy?" "Why can't a baby grow outside its mother, in a pouch like a kangaroo?"

Although children are constantly asking questions about birth, they may not want to know the answers. Alan asked how a daddy puts the seed inside a mommy. His mother tried to answer accurately. Mommy and Daddy love each other and they get close to each other in bed. Daddy has a special hole under his penis. "That's enough," Alan insisted. "I don't want to hear anymore."

Children who were adopted had their own concerns about birth. When Mike's mother told him that he was adopted, he asked her, "Does that mean I didn't come out of your tummy?" His mother explained that he had a birth mother who bore him, but she was his real mother. "But why," he asked, "didn't my birth mother want to keep me?" Karin also wanted to know more about her birth mother. "Where was she born? Can I visit her?"

Whether or not they are adopted, many children ask about their own birth. "How did I look when I was born? Was I crying? Was I a good baby?"

Death

Children between five and eight are concerned about, and often puzzled by, death. They wonder why people die, what happens after death, and whether death is inevitable. They are particularly concerned about the mortality of people around them, as well as about their own mortality.

Questions related to the reasons for death are common. When children ask about why people die, parents are likely to answer that people die when they get old. This answer seldom satisfies children, who may have a different concept of "old" than adults do. "Is Grandpa going to die because he's old?" asked Lisa. "Is fifty old?" asks Ned as his family makes plans for his father's upcoming birthday. "I don't want Dad to be old cause then he could die." Even more disturbing is when children hear about a younger person dying. "Remember that lady in the space shuttle? Why did she die? She wasn't that old, was she?" Jenna asked. "How can Dumpy be dead when he was just a puppy?" When children explain why a younger person or animal dies, whether or not the death was preventable, they associate the death with carelessness. Dumpy died because he ran into the road. Their friend Andrew died because he didn't take his medicine. Princess Diana died because she didn't wear her seat belt.

Another common concern of children is what happens after you die. Some children are interested in the details around death. "Did they put Grandpa in a casket?" "How come they put Aunt Lucy under the ground?" "What happens to Papa's bones?" A more prevalent concern is where you go after you die. No matter what they have been told by their parents, almost all children believe that there is a heaven. They want to know if cats and dogs go to heaven; if people can hear and see you once they are in heaven; if you can get people out of heaven if they don't want to stay there. Most of the time, children answer their own questions. Convinced his grandmother was being held in heaven by God against her will, Benjamin made an elaborate plan to construct a rope ladder to get his grandmother out. Darryl told his mother that his grandma looked down from heaven and watched him play center in the basketball game. Lisa insisted that Grandma Belle wasn't in heaven. Grandma was in Lisa's heart watching TV with her.

Many of the children in our sample were struggling with the idea that death is both irreversible and inevitable. When Katie's sister asked her what you do after you die, Katie said matter-of-factly, "You can't do anything, you're dead." While watching TV, Becky asked his mother if a favorite actor was dead. Her brother, Todd, answered immediately, "Of course he's dead, he just got shot." Becky's mother feels that Becky is still not quite clear about the difference between an actor being shot on the screen and an actor really dying. Jenna was upset when her great-grandmother died. "Is it true, Daddy," she asked, "that someday everybody has to die, even me?"

THE SOCIAL WORLD

Playing with Children Who Are Different

Although many children ask questions about children who are different, most children between five and eight are perfectly happy to play with children with different backgrounds or with different physical abilities. The questions that they ask reflect curiosity rather than bias. "Mommy, how come some children in my class can't read? Do you think they feel bad?" "Why are people different colors?" "I'm lucky, aren't I?" a white child asks. "My teacher is black." "I liked playing with my cousin. How come he has to stay in a wheelchair?" "Nana, do you know why I'm lucky? I was chosen for the friendship group and I got to be friends with a boy who has autism."

While some children are oblivious to differences in ethnicity, skin color, and handicapping conditions, other children notice the difference but do not assume that different means inferior or even that the difference is permanent. "I'm going to be black when I grow up," Darryl, a white kindergartner, told his teacher. "You are going to be what?" his teacher asked. "Black, I mean I'm going to have black skin." "How do you know?" "Because I'm going to be a famous basketball player, and famous basketball players are black."

Unfortunately, there are children from five to eight who are intolerant of differences. Some children tease children who are different, while other children are downright cruel. When Howard, a hearing-impaired boy, first entered an inclusive grade school, some of the children ganged up against him. They mocked his monotone voice and told him he sounded like a broken-down robot. Confused about how to handle this, Howard used his fists, and the jeering of the peer group escalated. Fortunately, the teacher was sensitive to the situation and knew how to handle it. She asked Howard to give an oral report on hearing impairment and show the children how hearing aids work. Howard made the presentation, and before long he was an accepted member of the class.

Leigh was teased mercilessly by her second-grade classmates when they found out she was adopted. All her parents' talk about how good it was to be a chosen child was to no avail. Leigh went home in tears. Her parents advised her to reply to their taunts by saying, "Yes, I am adopted," in a matter-of-fact tone. She took their advice and the teasing diminished. It wasn't nearly as much fun to tease Leigh when she didn't react with tears.

The World of Work

Work is exciting for elementary-age children. Children are curious about what their parents do at work and are happy to accompany their parents to a workplace. The connection between working, making money, and spending money, however, are difficult concepts to grasp. When Katie's mother wouldn't stop at a fast food restaurant because she didn't have money, Katie asked why she didn't go to the bank and get money or sell something at the mall. Kate asked her mother to buy her designer jeans. Her mother explained that they were just too expensive. "Then how come Ginny has designer jeans?" Kate asked. Her mother tried to explain. "Some families have more money than other families, but what really matters is not how much money you have but how much love there is in your home." Kate was not satisfied. "Well, if you don't have enough money to buy me jeans, you can just pay with a credit card."

Love, Marriage, and Sex

The questions children ask about love, sex, and marriage reflect both concerns around their own family and the influence of television. Many children want permission to marry one of their parents or to live in their parents' home after they are married. "Can I stay with you even if I am married?" "Why can't I marry Daddy?" "Do I really have to get married?" "Can you have children without getting married?"

Children also worry about the appropriateness of having a girlfriend at school, about using the correct terminology, and about breaking taboos against nudity. "Why do the children tease me when I call it a penis?" "Do I have to let Aunt Kate kiss me on my face?" "Those boys were bad, weren't they? They pulled down their pants and showed me their butt." "Why do they have that naughty stuff on television?" "Why does my cheerleader friend bring her boyfriend to the park? Does her mother know she has a boyfriend?" "Why do people kiss?" "Mommy, when you and Daddy were married, did he kiss your breast?" "Daddy, are you going out tonight? Are you going to have dinner at your girlfriend's house? Are you going to sleep there? Oh, oh, oh, Daddy!"

While some five-to-eight-year-olds are repelled by all that "smoochy" stuff, a few children are intrigued by sexual innuendoes and want to know more about sex. Much to Bobby's dismay, several of his friends scanned the web in order to see naked ladies. They also thumbed through magazines looking for "sexy" outfits. In actuality, the children were more interested in teasing Bobby and impressing each other than in looking at the pictures.

Understanding People

Children's questions about understanding people fall into two categories: "Why can't I" questions that relate to prohibitions or requests, and "How come" questions that reflect a need to make sense out of the world. The "Why can't I" type questions are familiar to every parent. "Why can't I have the same bedtime as my older brother?" "Why do you let Sarah get away with more things than you let me get away with when I was her age?" "Why can't we have a TV in the car?" "Why can't I have a baby brother or maybe a dog?"

Like the "Why can't I" questions, the "How come" questions are likely to be concerned with fairness. "How come that mother hit her child? You aren't supposed to do that." "Why does Daddy work so hard? He doesn't get to play with his children." "How come Andrew has a smaller house than I do?"

"How come there are street people and they don't have a house?" "How come some people in Jamaica have outhouses? Don't the children get scared at night when they have to go to the bathroom?" "How come some people are poor? Nothing in the world should cost money and then anyone could buy whatever they wanted to buy."

These "How come" questions often reflect both puzzlement and moral outrage. Marissa used her bedtime discussions with her mother to sort through these concerns. "Cara and Samia were being snobbish again today. I don't understand why they won't let Janelle play with us. They know it hurts her feelings."

World Events and Places

Curiosity about world events and places is sparked both by school studies and by watching television. The death of Princess Diana had a profound effect on many children and led to a barrage of questioning. "Why did Princess Diana die? Because she wasn't wearing her seat belt?" "Will Princess Diana's children be all right without a mother? How can they stand it? It's too sad." Some children who watch the news on TV with

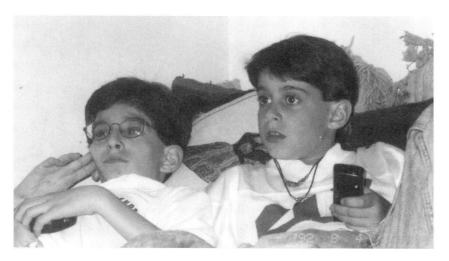

their parents want to understand what they are watching. "How do you get to be a president?" "The man who got shot is going to stay dead, 'cause the news is real, right?"

Violence and Disaster

Despite, or perhaps because of, their fear of violence, children are attracted to violent themes. They will turn just about anything into a gun, and question their parents' protestations against guns and fighting. "Mommy, why do we have to put away our guns? We're not killing people with our guns; we are just capturing bad men."

Children are quite willing to sing silly songs that have a violent theme. "I know an old woman who swallowed a fly. Perhaps she'll die." At the same time some children are upset by songs, videos, or movies when a significant character dies. Kevin wanted to change the Clementine song from "you are lost and gone forever," to "you are lost and we will find you," and to rewrite *The Lion King* so that Mufassa wouldn't die.

Real disasters that children watch on television can be especially disturbing. Several children became obsessed with Princess Diana's death. The fact that she was a mother with two children brought it too close to home. Pictures of children on television who were the victims of natural disasters had a similar effect. When a picture of children hurt in an earthquake was flashed on television, Kate turned off the set and ran out of the room. When Bobby watched a scene of families left homeless by a hurricane in Mexico, he gathered up a pile of toys that he wanted to send to the children.

Even though five-to-eight-year-olds understand that a disaster can't be undone, they can't always accept it. In question after question, they propose ways that the problem could have been averted, as if they somehow believe that there must be a way to make things right.

THE SUPERNATURAL WORLD

God, Heaven, and Religion

Many children between five and eight are struggling with the concept of God. By far the greatest number of questions reflect a need to understand what God is really like. "Where is God?" "Is God a man or a woman?" "Does God let dogs into heaven?" "Does God get hungry? Does he sleep?" Asked what God is, Justin carries on a debate with himself. "You mean, is God alive or not? Well, I don't think he's alive because then he would be speaking and we would hear it. He wasn't ever alive because God never dies so he was never alive. He could be like a genie, a magical human with lots of power over everything. He's very big. But remember, I didn't say he was alive."

A related set of questions comes out of a need to square religious teachings with information about history and the physical world. "Is the Garden of Eden in New York or in Israel?" "Where did Jesus fall in with the dinosaurs?" "God has been there since the beginning of time and he won't ever die. Time began when there was a big bang, right?"

The kinds of questions about God that children ask seem to be age related. Five-to-six-year-olds think about God as a person who can either punish or reward you. "Is God a nice guy?" "Will God put me in the bad book or the good book?" Some of their questions about God and religion reflect children's confusion about things they have been told. "How could Adam not have a mother?" "Were there cavemen in the Garden of Eden?" "Who is Satan?" "Who was Jesus?" "Why do people believe in Jesus?" "Does Jesus believe in God?" "If God didn't make me, would you still love me?"

Many of the questions asked by six-to-seven-year-olds reflect a concern about heaven and hell. "Where is heaven and where is hell? Why can't we see them?" "How high is heaven?" "When dogs die do they go to heaven?" "Is O. J. Simpson going to hell?" "Mommy, if you go to heaven I want to go, but if you go to hell I don't want to go there with you."

Some seven- and eight-year-old children express skepticism about God. "Who is God?" "Why do we have to pray to him?" "Why do we have to go to church?" "Has anyone ever seen God? Then maybe he is just a hypothesis."

It is not unusual for five-to-eight-year-old children to ask questions about other religions. For the most part, these questions revolve around the celebration of holidays. Mark told his mother that he knew he was Jewish and Jewish children don't believe in Santa Claus, but couldn't Santa just come to *their* house? Leigh announced that she would like to be Christian so that Santa Claus would bring her family presents. Marvin's parents were having trouble getting their Christmas tree to stand up. After it fell down for the third time, Marvin asked why they couldn't just celebrate Chanukah.

Although most children limited their interest in other religions to holidays and presents, there were some exceptions. Kevin wanted his mother to tell him about Jesus Christ. Christopher told his mother that he didn't like going to church. "They are always telling me things I don't understand. Why can't we be a different religion?" After helping her friend put up a Christmas tree, Brooke asked her mother why people couldn't be both Jewish and Christian. Alice, who is Buddhist, makes holiday cards for friends who are Christian and Jewish. Curious about different religious practices, she hounds her parents for information. She took her neighbors apples and honey for the Jewish New Year, and was thrilled when they invited her to stay for the ritual meal.

Santa Claus and the Tooth Fairy

Santa Claus

Most five- and six-year-olds believe that Santa Claus is real, and their questions are requests for explanations rather than a concern about his existence. "Where does Santa live?" "How does he get down the chimney?" "Are all Santas in the department stores Santa's helpers, or are they dressed-up men?" "How come Santa Claus doesn't bring Mrs. Claus along?"

As children mature they may hold onto their belief in Santa Claus, but their questions reflect their doubts. "Why do parents buy presents if Santa does?" "How could anybody live for hundreds of years in the North Pole?" "How could he get to all the houses in the world on the same night? Do you think he freezes time?"

The Tooth Fairy

The tooth fairy is important to five- and six-year-olds. It makes the loss of a tooth a cause for celebration. Children quite frequently write notes to the tooth fairy. "Dear Tooth Ferry—I am hapy you came. Leave me muny.—Becky." When Kate lost her

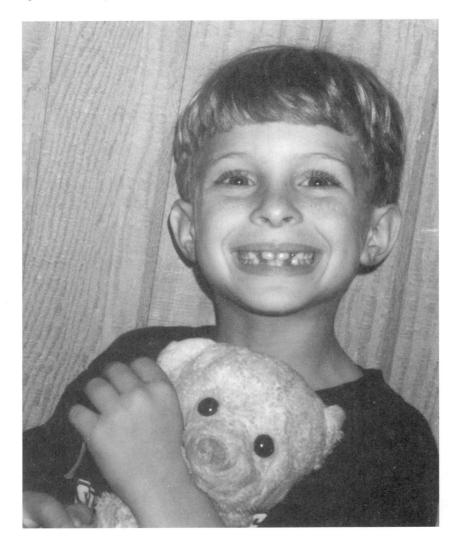

tooth down the drain, she drew a picture of a tooth and put it under her pillow. When Crystal's father forgot to put money under her pillow, she was content with the explanation that the tooth fairy was running a bit late. Crystal went back to sleep, and sure enough the tooth fairy put a dollar under her pillow.

Ever since Kori lost her first tooth, she had been exchanging notes with the tooth fairy. Through these notes, they had become great friends. When Kori asked the tooth fairy for a picture of herself, the tooth fairy explained that she was invisible, and gave Kori a book about the power of belief, explaining, "This is like a picture of the inside of me." Kori loved the exchanges, and held on to her belief in the tooth fairy as long as she could. Finally, at eight, Kori was no longer confident that the tooth fairy was real. She confronted her mother: "Mom, tell me the truth. Did you write that note?" "Kori, before I answer that, tell me what you hope I will say." "I hope you'll say you didn't but I know you'll say you did because the writing looks just like yours." "Well, Kori, I did write the note. But I didn't write it as me. When I write for the tooth fairy, I turn myself into the tooth fairy; I become the character just like you do when you talk for your dolls or write a story. So really, the tooth fairy wrote the note." This explanation satisfied Kori, allowing her to keep both her relationship with a cherished friend and her new scientific appreciation of the difference between real and pretend.

Like Kori, many children, especially the seven- or eight-year-olds, have their doubts about the existence of a tooth fairy. "How would the tooth fairy know where everyone lived?" "She is so little, how could she deliver the gifts?" "How could she get in the house when the alarm is on?" At the same time, it is a beautiful fantasy that they do not want to give up.

ANSWERS TO PARENTS' QUESTIONS

What can I do to help maintain my child's curiosity?

Continue to take time answering your child's questions. Your interest and responsiveness will spark her curiosity and encourage her to make new discoveries that she can share with you. At the same time, capitalize on your child's emerging interests and provide books and real-life experiences that will expand her knowledge base. Another way to maintain your child's curiosity is to share your own questions with your child. If she is interested in your questions, you and your child can research plausible answers.

My child's misconceptions are cute, but should I correct them?

It is better not to ignore misconceptions even though they are fun to listen to. Often a child's questions are presented as a statement. "White clouds make snow and dark clouds make rain, right?" Your child is expecting a confirmation or an explanation. Allowing the misconception to go unchallenged will be interpreted by your child as a confirmation. It is important, however, to assure your child that his explanation is interesting and makes a lot of sense.

I'm not entirely comfortable with the way I answered my child's questions about how the baby got inside me. Can you give me some guidance?

All parents struggle to find an appropriate answer to questions about conception. Unfortunately there are no pat answers for every situation and for every child. A good rule of thumb is to answer every question truthfully but with the simplest possible explanation. "How does a baby get started?" "It grows from an egg in a mother's uterus." Do not volunteer further information unless your child asks for it. If your child asks about the father's role, answer simply but honestly. "The father makes sperm that join with the egg that is in the mother."

If your child continues to ask questions about how a baby is born, it might be helpful to find a book about birth that explains the process in words that your child can understand. Avoid books that begin with the birds and bees. Your child is likely to lose interest before you get to the babies. When you talk to or read to your child about how babies are born, don't make the assumption that he knows nothing about it. By seven or eight, most children know something about intercourse, including slang words. However, they are likely not to have made the connection between having intercourse and having a baby.

My child says he wants to be a doctor like my husband when he grows up. Do many children know what they want to be? Is it a good idea to encourage good choices?

Very few children know what they want to be when they grow up. Many children between five and eight talk about what they are going to be when they grow up. For some children, this interest is transitory. When Kevin was planning out his inventions, he decided to become a scientist. When he got involved in building things, he decided that he would become a factory worker. Darryl had always talked about becoming a pharmacist like his father. One day, however, when his mother explained that they could not get a giant-screen TV because it was too expensive, Darryl announced that he was going to be a banker when he grew up.

Unlike Kevin and Darryl, some five-to-eight-year-olds develop enduring interests. Children who like to take care of babies might grow up to be a teacher, doctor, or social worker. Children who like to take things apart might grow up to be a mechanic or a scientist. Children who are always building things might become carpenters or engineers. Children who have a range of interests may develop lifelong hobbies that could become careers. Mrs. Halpern, a second-grade teacher, talked about one child named Gail who loved to paint and whose parents built her a studio. She couldn't predict whether or not Gail would end up being an artist, but she was pleased that her parents recognized and encouraged her creative talent.

When a child like Gail shows a strong interest or talent, it is important for parents to give her an opportunity to explore her interest or express her talent. At the same time, parents need to be careful about waxing too enthusiastic if their child makes a career choice that pleases them. By the time our five-to-eight-year-olds grow up, there will be new choices that we may not even imagine today.

Is it too early to teach kids the facts of life, not just about sex but about things like work, money, and social class?

It is never too early to discuss a topic in which children have shown interest. Resist the temptation of telling your child more than he can understand or more than he wants to hear. It is never a good idea to begin a discussion on work, money, or social class out of context. If your child objects to your going to work, it is a good opportunity to explain to your child that you have to go to work to earn money for the family. If your child is curious about why the school is collecting money for buying Thanksgiving turkeys for poor people, it is a good opportunity to talk about children who are needy.

Listen to the kinds of questions that your child asks and answer those questions. Do not give your child a lecture on economics. If your child asks a potentially embarrassing question, such as whether you make more money than a friend's parent or why her house is larger or smaller than theirs, it is best to be honest. At the same time, you can remind your child that people generally don't talk about how much money they have because that is considered private. Five-to-eight-year-olds are busy comparing themselves with peers along many dimensions. They don't always have to be at the top, but they like to know where they fit in. Children who develop empathy for people who are in need are not likely to demand things from their parents that they cannot afford, or be unkind to children whose families are not well off.

When are children old enough to watch the news?

It is better to talk with children about the news or give them selected articles to read than to encourage them to watch the news. Children understand that news is real and that people who get shot on the news are not just actors. The more sensational the news, the more frightened your child may become. You may want to invite your children to watch selected programs that describe news events.

When he is a little older and less likely to be frightened, you can invite your child to watch the news with you. Then, if your child is upset by some sensational news, you can always switch to another channel.

My child is getting interested in religion, and I'd like to teach her more. But I don't want to impose my beliefs on her, and I'm not sure how to deal with the negative and violent parts, like Christ dying on a cross or God destroying the world with a flood.

It is possible and appropriate to teach children about religion without going into all aspects of its history. It is also important for parents to share their belief systems with their child. Do not be afraid of imposing your beliefs. As your child gets older, she will question you about aspects of religion that she finds confusing or illogical.

Should I worry about a child who doesn't believe in Santa Claus, the tooth fairy, or anything magical?

Somewhere between five and eight, most children question the existence of Santa Claus and the tooth fairy. They are also likely to discover that the feats of a magician are tricks. This does not mean that a child does not enjoy or appreciate magic. Knowing that a story or a movie is just a fairy tale does not take away its appeal for adults, and certainly will not for children.

Should I worry that my child won't let go of his belief in Santa, even though all of his friends have outgrown it?

The idea of there being a Santa Claus is very appealing to children. Some children hold on to their belief in Santa Claus longer than others. Even though they may suspect that their parents are the real givers of gifts, it is not unusual for children even beyond eight years old to continue to believe that Santa Claus really exists.

PLAY IDEAS

- Even before your child can read, you can take her to the library and help her find books that answer her questions. Encourage her to ask more questions as she looks at the pictures in books or as you read to her.
- Include "question time" as part of your child's bedtime or mealtime ritual. If your child can't think of a question to ask you, provide a model. "You know what I wonder about? How do they make cereal crispy?" Encourage both fanciful and factual questions about the natural, human, physical, and supernatural worlds. If you don't know an answer, speculate together. How many plausible answers can you think of? Your child will most likely be eager to look up the answer and find out which one, or ones, are right.
- Help your child investigate answers to her own questions, especially recurring ones, using a range of sources. What people are most likely to know the answer? Can you find experts at stores, museums, or church? Is there a person or

company you can write to? What books or reference books might tell? What can you find on the Internet, in videos, or on TV?

- Trips and outings often provoke interesting questions. Share your own observations and questions with your child, and take time to tune into hers. Extend the trip with books or videos that provide more information about the things that most interested your child.

- Encourage your child to look at familiar things from a new perspective. What would a baby find to play with in your kitchen? What would be dangerous? What would a dog notice on the way to school? What would a bird or butterfly notice?

- Keep track of your child's more unusual questions and misconceptions, especially those you can't answer or can't explain in a way that she can grasp. A month or a year later, you may discover new information that relates to the question. Or reminding her of what she once thought, you may discover how her thinking has changed.

- Help your child understand the difference between questions that have one right answer, questions that different people answer differently, and questions that we don't yet know the answers to.

- Play Twenty Questions with your children. You might start by saying, "I am thinking of an animal." Children may start by guessing the names of animals, but before long they will discover that it is more efficient to ask more general questions that will narrow the field. "Is it a human being?" "Does it live on the land?" "Is it bigger than a cat?" "Is it a mammal?" "Does it live in the forest?"

- Play Question Box with your children. Give each child a color. Write questions on different color index cards, making sure that the questions on each different color card are appropriate for the child who has been assigned that color.

Children are allowed to keep the question cards they have answered correctly. Join in the game by letting the children write out questions for you. Don't be surprised if they think of questions where they know the answer and you don't.

- Place some objects in a box. Let each child take out the first object he touches. The other players ask for three hints about the object, for example, what is the object for? The child who is holding the object tries to find a way of answering the question without giving away the answer. For example, if the child who has selected a paper clip is asked what it's for, she could answer, "To attach something to something else."

- Pretend you are going on a trip to a place that is familiar to your children. Give the children two or three hints. See if they can guess where you are pretending to go. Give your children a turn to pretend to go on a trip and give you three hints.

- Give your children the answer and see if they can guess the question, for example, "They are extinct."

- If your child is wavering between believing and not believing in Santa Claus or the tooth fairy, write notes from the tooth fairy or Santa to your child. Your child will recognize your handwriting but will realize how much fun it can be holding on to a belief even though he knows it is a fantasy.

CHAPTER 3

Friends

~~~~~~

I will not play with Jimmy.
I will not play at all.
He always says it's his turn first,
And then he hogs the ball.

He tells me that I'm his best friend
And we will never part.
Then he goes off and plays with Jeff
And nearly breaks my heart.

For most five-to-eight-year-olds, the world revolves around their friends. When friends are getting along, the world is sunny and life is great. When your best friend abandons you or you are rejected by the group, nothing seems to go right. Whether your friend is a peer, a sibling, or an adult, having someone to play with makes any play more fun.

In this chapter we look at children's relationships with best friends, at how children resolve controversies and conflicts, and at issues of inclusion and exclusion, including cliques, clubs, triangles, and status within the group. We then discuss sibling relationships and friendships with adults.

BEST FRIENDS

Making and keeping good friends is the key to success in grade school. For most children it is more important to have friends than to get good grades or to win the admiration of a teacher. In preschool, a friend is a playmate who shares your play ideas. In grade school, a friend becomes a trusted companion and you are always there for each other. You share feelings as well as your play ideas. Being with your friend enhances your sense of security and gives you a feeling of well-being.

In general, children in the five-to-eight-year-old age range select a best friend or best friends of the same gender. This can be attributed, at least in part, to the fact that boys and girls prefer different kinds of activities. Many girls love intimate friendships, where they sit together in a private place, whispering and giggling and sharing secrets. Other girls enjoy being a part of a small group, playing out a pretend theme, or putting on a performance. Boys, on the other hand, enjoy more active play. Even with their best friends at hand they like to play in a larger group.

While grade-school children select same-sex children, girls and boys do not always go their separate ways. Five-year-olds play with both girls and boys. They refer to their same-sex friends as best friends, and their opposite-sex friends as boyfriend or girlfriend. Some five-year-old girl–boy pairs will arrange a wedding and consider themselves to be a married couple. J. T. explained to his mother one day that Candy was really his wife because they had had seven weddings.

Like five-year-olds, six-year-olds may have boyfriends or girlfriends, although their best friends usually are of the same sex. Girls are likely to choose as boyfriends boys who are not aggressive or mean.

Katie, at six years old, has two best boyfriends, Bobby and Luis. One day she came home from school complaining that

her nose hurt. Those mean boys had kicked a ball right into her face, but, she assured her mother, "it wasn't Bobby or Luis who did it."

Although six-, seven-, and eight-year-olds play in segregated groups, some of this separation is not as consistent with children who are eight years old. Boys declare that they hate girls, and girls declare that they hate boys, but their actions belie their words.

Siri and Elena were on the playground twirling hula hoops. A group of boys standing nearby kept edging over to the girls. "Pretty sexy there," one of the boys shouted to no one in particular. "Bug off, stupid heads," the girls shouted back. "Who do you think you are calling a stupid head?" The girls and boys continued parlaying back and forth, and despite the escalation of insults, they were obviously enjoying each other.

Leigh, age eight, had a group of girlfriends in Sunday school. During recess on a rainy day her class went into the social hall. At Leigh's instigation, the girls chased the boys

around the room. Leigh's friend picked up a chair and shouted out, "It's a bar mitzvah!" She sat on the chair and challenged the boys to lift the chair into the air. Despite some back-and-forth teasing, Leigh and her friends had a great time playing with the boys.

Initiating Friendships

The different ways in which children initiate friendships is fascinating to watch. There is a distinct age-related difference in friend-making techniques. Five-year-olds make friends by sharing an activity or playing with the same toy. Six-year-olds are likely to select best friends from the "pool" of children they had played with in earlier years. Friendship is cemented by pre-planned play. Quite often, children will meet each other before school and plan to play together at recess or sit together during class. Prearranged play dates are particularly popular with six-year-olds. Kevin, at six years old, planned his schedule a week

in advance so that each of his friends could have their turn coming to his house for a play date. "But I can't go to the dentist," Kevin explained to his mother. "It's Karl's turn to come to the house and I don't want to hurt his feelings."

Seven- and eight-year-olds are likely to hold onto friendships established in earlier grades. At the same time, they may develop a repertoire of strategies for initiating new friendships. These range from straightforward invitations to play to more subtle attempts to establish a connection by finding a common bond. On a trip to Peru to visit his grandparents, Xavier went to a restaurant in Lima that featured Peruvian music and dancing. A young girl who happened to be dressed in an aquamarine dress that matched Xavier's shirt was standing in front of the dance floor. Xavier's parents suggested that he go up to her and introduce himself. Xavier, who tended to be shy in this kind of situation, finally agreed to go up to the dance floor. Two minutes later he was holding hands with the girl, and five minutes later they were walking arm in arm around the restaurant. "I feel as if I have known her from a long time ago," Xavier told his parents.

Loss of a Best Friend

When best friends move away or change schools, children may be traumatized. Brittany's best friend, Leslie, moved out of town. They used to play dress-up, put on shows, and pass out tickets to a parent audience. At first, after Leslie left, Brittany went through a period of mourning. After a few months she started making friends, but they were not really soul mates.

Heather, like Brittany, had a best friend who moved out of town. Heather was a shy, sensitive child, who was ignored rather than disliked. When Aliza lived in town, the two friends spent every weekend sleeping over at one of their homes. Heather and Aliza had developed an elaborate play routine that involved rescuing their dolls from a faraway country and giving them a safe home. When Aliza left, Heather was devastated. She was accepted as a low status member of a play group at school but was never able to find another Aliza.

Ned's best friend Sam did not move out of town, but when Sam went to a different elementary school Ned lost his exclusive relationship with Sam. Ned and Sam had been bosom pals in nursery school, but Sam, an easygoing child, made lots of new friends. He is often unavailable for after-school play, and Ned, even in the second grade, is reluctant to accept substitutes. His early friendship with Sam had been special. Ned was always bigger and braver, and Sam always looked up to him. When Ned would invite him to play at his house after school, Sam would watch Ned show off his Nintendo skills without needing a turn. When Sam and Ned went together to Spooky World recently, Ned, living up to his reputation as the "tough" one, went into all the places where Sam was afraid to go himself. (In actuality, Ned was also afraid, but he didn't admit it to anyone until he was safe at home.) When Ned and Sam get a chance to play by themselves, they play happily for hours without conflict, drifting easily from soccer to drawing to fort building to street hockey or baseball. They get along equally well in public, when their families get together or when they play on the same team. Occasionally, however, Ned will be unable to contain his jealousy and will say something mean to Sam. Ned has found other children to play with in school, but he hasn't made a real friend there. In Ned's mind, there just isn't anyone like Sam.

CONTROVERSIES AND CONFLICTS

Having one or more best friends is critically important to most five-to-eight-year-old children. At the same time, there is a downside. Children are more likely to quarrel with a best friend than with casual friends. They are also more likely to get into a triangle situation where a third child threatens a best-friend relationship. Just as hurtful, best friends can form cliques or initi-ate clubs that exclude other children.

"If you won't give me a turn, I won't be your best friend." "If you won't give me that ball, I won't invite you to my birth-day." These are common phrases with preschool children. Chil-dren five to eight are less likely to use these particular phrases, but having a best friend and being invited to a best friend's birthday party are still of prime importance.

Jenna's feelings were hurt because she thought that one of her best friends, Amanda, did not invite her to her birthday party. Despite her mother's sound advice, Jenna decided to in-vite everyone except Amanda to her birthday party. Amanda and Jenna's mothers were friends. Apparently Amanda's mother was terribly hurt because her daughter was excluded from the birthday party, although she thought it was just an oversight. Jenna's mother admitted that Jenna had made a de-liberate decision not to invite Amanda because Amanda hadn't invited her to her party. "But Amanda didn't have a party!" her mother exclaimed. When Jenna's mother reported the conver-sation, Jenna was apologetic. Without a prompt from her

mother, she picked up the telephone, told Amanda she was terribly sorry, and invited her to come to the party.

Rifts within the Peer Group

While best-friend rifts are particularly painful, children can also be hurt when any of their peers are mean or rejecting. Hurt feelings are generated in many common situations. A child refuses to share a toy or give another child a turn on the swing. A child cheats in a game and then boasts about being the winner. A child organizes a performance and refuses to let another child be the princess. A child teases another child about the color of her skin, her size, or the way she is dressed.

Katie was going swimming with her class. Her mother had forgotten to give her a towel, but she dropped a Barney towel off at the school later in the day. Katie picked up the towel and went to the swim class. When the other children saw the Barney towel, they teased her about being a baby, and Katie, as you would predict, was mortified.

Caroline was playing on the playground when Amy, another eight-year-old, decided she wanted a partner to play with. Several children refused to play with her, but Caroline went over to her and volunteered to be her partner. Amy, who was obviously in a bad mood, snapped at Caroline. "I'd rather be alone than play with you." Although Caroline told the story to her mother, she didn't seem too disturbed. Sometimes children can be more forgiving than adults.

Resolving Conflicts with Peers

Conflicts with peers are inevitable, and in actuality they serve a purpose. Because children want to have friends to play with, they are motivated to find ways of resolving the conflict. Over time, they learn to see each other's point of view, to defend

their own point of view, to use words and not hands, to resolve problems, to negotiate, to compromise, and to reach equitable solutions. Children, of course, are not always capable of resolving conflicts on their own. Sometimes they expect a parent or a teacher to resolve their conflict, and sometimes parents or teachers intervene before children have had the opportunity to work it out on their own.

Five-year-olds are likely to resolve a conflict by resuming their play after a short break. Sarah and Lisa quarreled about who could be the teacher in a classroom they set up with their dolls. They shouted at each other for a while and then went out in the backyard by what appeared to be mutual consent. A few minutes later they were swinging together on the backyard swing, and the conflict was completely forgotten. Like five-year-olds, six-to-eight-year-olds may sometimes get into a physical fight or a verbal battle, but unlike five-year-olds, they usually don't consider the conflict over until one or both children apologize. Here are some strategies that were used successfully by children six to eight to solve a conflict and avert a rift.

Kevin reported to his mother that a kid in school bullied him. His mother asked him how he handled it. Kevin answered that he had a talk with the boy. "I told him I don't like it and that was not the way to act. Now we are good friends." Brittany had a similar problem with a girl at school who was always bossing her around. "Tell her that you like playing with her, but you don't like it when she bosses you around," suggested her mother. "I couldn't say that!" countered Brittany. "That's what a grown-up would say. I'll just say, 'Don't boss me. I like you, but I don't like bossing.'"

Justin described a fight that he had at school. "We made a club in school and then some kid made a different club. He put antennae on his head and made a club of bug people. And we were fighting them and I got whacked and it hurt." "Were you having fun or were you angry with each other?" his mother asked. "We were having fun, but it hurt. We weren't angry. We're friends now cause they know if they fight me I can whip them."

Katie told her mother that she was upset because a friend in her class said she was too slow. "What did you do about it?" her mother asked. "Oh, I just went faster," Katie answered nonchalantly.

Kevin was talking to his mother about his friends at school. "I really would like to play with Todd because he's fun, but John gets upset when I play with someone else. So you know what I did? I played with Todd, but we kept it a secret. John sometimes says mean things when he gets mad at me, but I know he doesn't mean it. We are really good friends."

Eight-year-old Caroline was playing with her best friend, Alexandra. The girls decided to play "detective" but "got into a fight" because they both wanted to be named Ashley. They resolved the problem in an interesting way. Caroline started writing a letter to Alexandra, who looked over her shoulder and then copied the idea. Both letters consisted of a series of questions, such as the following: "Do you want to make up?" "Will you still be my friend?" "Am I still your best friend?" Of course, all the answers were yes, and both girls were thrilled, although they almost got in another fight over who would apologize first. The rituals of "fighting" and "making up," although bringing serious tears, were also a form of play. Caroline enjoyed retelling the story, using her "pretending" or "storytelling" voice. The girls seemed to be rehearsing conflict and resolution, breaking and mending relationships in play.

In some situations, children are unable or not given the opportunity to resolve a conflict on their own. Parents use different techniques to restore the peace. Karin's mother felt that the best way to avoid conflict was to establish rules. Karin and her friend were arguing about whether they should play with Nintendo or build a haunted house. As soon as the argument began Karin's mother stepped in. "Remember," she told her daughter, "friends always get first choice when they are playing at our house."

Angela's mother felt that her daughter was too inflexible and used mild punishment to resolve a dispute. "When Angela has a friend over, she always wants things her own way. If she doesn't get her way she refuses to play. I just put her in time-out."

INCLUSION AND EXCLUSION

Cliques

According to their teachers, children in the five-to-eight age range become increasingly "cliquey" as they go through the grades. A clique, as defined by the teachers, is a loosely structured but closely knit group who are usually seen together and who exclude other children. Members of a clique often have a common interest that solidifies the group. It may be a status symbol like clothes, athletic trophies, or their parents' cars, or a particular interest like rap, the opposite sex, or certain after-school activities.

Cliques have a way of bringing out both the best and the worst in children. Being a member of a clique makes children feel socially secure. They never have to be concerned about having someone to play with or talk to. Friends are always available, to laugh with, share secrets with, and spend good times

with. At the same time, cliques have negative effects. Children gossip about other children, make unkind or downright mean remarks, and purposely ignore other children who are not members of the "inner circle." Unfortunately, the cohesiveness of the clique is often maintained by its negative behaviors.

Pilar, an attractive but somewhat shy girl, was transferred to a new school in the middle of a semester. She left home with trepidation, feeling that she wouldn't know anyone in the new school and wouldn't be able to make friends. Her mother told her to watch for a group of children that she would like to know. "Introduce yourself, and tell them that this is your first day at school and you don't know your way around." Pilar took her mother's advice and went up to a group of girls who were on their way to the playground. The girls liked the idea of being in a helpful role, and with no hesitation accepted Pilar into their clique.

Kathleen, who was always dressed in neat jerseys or shirts despite the sloppy shirt style that was in vogue at the school, became the butt of the jokes of one of the cliques. In an attempt to win their favor, Kathleen passed out a piece of candy to each member of the clique. The girls accepted the candy, but as she walked off they whispered loudly enough so that she could hear it, "'Missy, sissy, prissy, give me a kissy." Kathleen left the scene in tears.

Triangle Situations

Kevin: "Okay, John, let's go out and dig worms from under the fence. I know a real good spot."

John: "I don't want to."

Kevin: "Come on, it's fun."

John: "I don't want to play with you."

Kevin: "How come?"

John: " 'Cause yesterday you played with Todd all day, and I'm s'posed to be your best friend."

Triangle situations are the most likely source of conflict for children five to eight. The old adage that "two's company, three's a crowd" is a good description for many elementary-school relationships. As with John and Kevin, when one best friend decides to play with another child, the child left behind can suffer pangs of jealousy.

Bobby had trouble with one friend who was particularly possessive and didn't want him to play with any other friend. Bobby explained to his friend that he didn't want to hurt her feelings but that he liked to play with other friends, too. "You can always join in when I am playing with other friends." At the end of the conversation both children hugged and cried and were best of friends again.

Clubs

Five-to-eight-year-olds are particularly fond of creating clubs. Very little actually happens in a club, but it does give children a chance to feel included in a group, while excluding other children. Clubs are not the same as cliques. A club is always given a name, which in some way is related to its purpose. Eight-year-olds may develop criteria for membership in the club and may use a promise of membership as a way of getting something that they want.

Caroline, at eight years old, wanted to be accepted into the Hip Clothes Club. At first she was rejected outright, but then the children decided that she could join the club if she would invite them to her house and let them borrow her brothers' hip clothes. Caroline did not want to comply, but she did tell her brothers the whole sad story on the way home from school. Her brother Greg had a solution. "You know what, Caroline? There are a whole lot of us. Let's start up our own Hip Clothes Club!"

In contrast to cliques, clubs are likely to have criteria for membership. Some clubs are open only to members who have

name-brand sneakers. Other clubs are open to members who are willing to get into mischief. The club that Justin belonged to had made a firm decision to keep out girls. However, on Justin's insistence one girl was invited to join their Secret Service Club.

"I have four friends," Justin told us. "We started up the Secret Service Club for boys only, and it even has officers. But then there's this girl, she's a midget, she's only this tall, and she's my best friend so we let her join even though she's a girl. We made her an officer dog."

Group Play

Groups are quite different from cliques or clubs. Children join a play group in order to participate in an activity. In boys' groups the play is likely to be action-packed, with one child assuming a leadership role. Children are seldom excluded from the group, although some children have higher status than others. When girls gather together in groups, they may begin by running and chasing but are likely to end up putting on a performance or acting out a pretend play theme. The decision to include or exclude another child is often relegated to the leader of the group.

The first graders in an elementary school were going to the playground. Having decided to play "Dracula," a group of girls rushed over to the climbing structure for a secret meeting. After they had settled the problem of who should be Dracula by deciding that they all could be Dracula, the performance began. "I am the great Mother Dracula. Who wants to dance

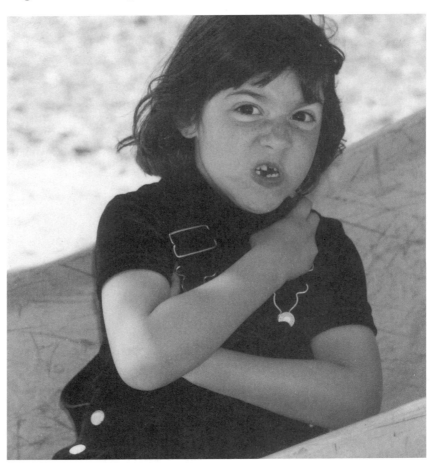

with me?" "No," one girl interrupted, "Draculas aren't sup-posed to dance. They are just supposed to be scary." "Well then, we'll do a scary dance," a third child suggested. "No way," insisted "Mother Dracula," who called the shots. "First we'll make scary noises, and then do our scary Dracula mon-ster dance." As the play continued, several new children joined in the group.

While the girls put on their Dracula performance, a large group of boys ran to the far side of the playground. They chased each other around the "bases" several times, swinging their arms and making "Hoopalah" noises. Next they tossed a ball back and forth, gathered up twigs and staged a pretend fight. According to the teachers, the same group of boys came to the same part of the playground every time they had a recess. For the most part, their play was disorganized, with several children running in and out of the group.

A group of grade school teachers, meeting to discuss the group play they had observed on the playground, generated this list of generalizations:

- Boys' groups are larger than girls' groups.
- Girls' popularity is more likely to be based on the creativity of their play ideas, while boys value athletic prowess.
- Boys are more competitive and girls are more bossy.
- Boys are likely to spend their recess time running around the playground, throwing balls at each other, or pretending they are robots, space monsters, or *Star Wars* characters.
- Girls are more likely to gather in small groups, stage a perfor-mance, or engage in pretend family play.

The teachers also pointed out some differences based on age:

- Kindergarten children move fluidly from group to group.
- First- and second-grade children stay with one group consis-tently, although some children move in intimate twosomes.

- By second grade, groups are established, and there is little rejection.
- As children get older the pecking order is more strongly established. There are low-status, middle-status, and high-status children, and once you are pegged it is difficult to change your status.
- Third-grade children play organized games and are intent on establishing and following the rules.

A favorite recess game described by the teachers was where third graders played baseball without a ball or a bat. They pretended to throw, hit, and catch an imaginary ball, and raced at top speed from base to base. Apparently the children had established some game rules, but the teacher couldn't fathom what they were.

Floaters and Bridge Builders

As children's groups solidify, there are usually a few children who refuse to be pigeonholed. Some, like Sonia, are "floaters," playing with one friend or group one day and another friend or group the next day. As Sonia explains to her mother, "I like Ollie because he's a really a good basketball player and he runs really fast. I like Jamal because he's a good reader like me. I like to listen to Rebecca tell stories. Conor is funny, so I like to play with him, too."

Sonia's older sister, Marissa, also likes to play with children who are very different from each other. But Marissa is less likely than Sonia to simply take turns. Instead, she finds ways to bring children with different interests together, inventing games and projects in which they can all participate.

James is another example of a bridge builder. At school, he considers himself the "shy guy," and usually goes along with whichever group invites him in. As soon as he gets home, however, James dashes to the phone. He calls up all the kids in the neighborhood and organizes the afternoon play. Depending on the weather and the number of kids he can recruit, he may organize a baseball or soccer game in the park, a fishing expedition to the local pond, a neighborhood walk or bike ride, or a backyard barbecue. Fortunately, his parents don't mind feeding the whole neighborhood on a regular basis.

Status with Peers

Teachers who were familiar with group dynamics identified the following characteristics in children that determined their status with their peers.

• Children who are well-liked by their classmates are self-confident, playful, and full of good ideas. They also are good organizers, know how to mobilize a group, and can keep the play from breaking down.

- Children who are accepted in the group, but not as leaders, are apt to be flexible, relaxed, unconcerned about being the boss, and perfectly happy to follow the leader.

- Children who are on the fringes of groups, sometimes invited in and sometimes not, are usually children who are independent, shy, gentle, and often very bright or creative.

- Children who are rejected by the group are likely to be socially awkward, trying to force themselves into the group by being bossy, acting silly, or picking on more vulnerable children. These children appear to be generally unhappy and out of touch. They want to play with the group but they don't know how.

Loners

A few children are genuine loners. Allison, at five and a half, was one of these children. On her way out to the playground, she said "Hi" to two children and went directly to the swings. When another child arrived, Allison gave him the swing and went over to the sandbox. She busied herself patting down the

rather wet sand, made a cake, and wrote her name on top of it. Two children came over and started building similar cakes. Allison said goodbye to the twosome and went over to the jungle gym. It was quite clear that Allison, although perfectly friendly, preferred to be alone. Allison's teacher was unconcerned because Allison was both happy and socially adept. When she chose to join a group or play with a friend, Allison did so with ease. Because she was so good-natured about it, the other children accepted Allison's frequent need to play by herself.

SIBLING PLAY

Jessica and Susan are close in age and, because they are home-schooled, spend a lot of time together. Their favorite activity is dress-up. They love to dress up as storybook characters, collect appropriate props, and have their parents guess who they are.

Sonia, age six, and her sister Marissa, who just turned nine, are constantly discovering new activities that they both enjoy. On some days they play with miniature characters, taking great pains to distribute the characters so that each child has the same number. Once the distribution is completed they arrange the characters into families and play out a pretend theme. They also enjoy playing card games, such as Frog Juice,

Rat-a-Tat, Slamwich, and Spit. When their mother agrees to do the taping, the girls love to make their own videos. They make tickets for the show, select costumes, sing songs, and make up dances, bowing to an imaginary audience at the end of each performance.

Endre enjoys playing with his older sister Marie and doesn't mind it when she bosses him around. Bedtime is a special time for the siblings. They shut their door and talk and laugh for at least a half hour each night, enjoying their private world.

While siblings may have a great time playing with each other, they also get into scraps. Sonia and Marissa run into problems when Marissa introduces "bad guys" into Sonia's families, schools, circuses, or hospitals. Katie, who usually plays well with her older sister, gets annoyed when Rachel selects the radio station in the car. "You are hurting my feelings. You are being mean. You always get your way. You always get to choose the station on the radio. It's not fair!" Alice, who most of the time tags happily along behind her big sister, quarrels with her over who is going to sit by Mommy or who is going to get the favored place mat. Bobby and his brother ordinarily get along with each other but argue vehemently over whose turn it is to use the computer.

Ethan, who is six years old, is constantly telling his younger brother what to do. When Eric doesn't follow directions Ethan gets frustrated. "Eric, you are ruining everything. Get out of my room." Because Eric so much wants to be in his

big brother's orbit, sending him away seldom works for long. Recently, Ethan has learned to trick Eric into playing with a less favored toy or doing a job that can't be botched, such as making a block garage for the lego model he's building.

Although siblings hassle with each other over a whole host of things, the underlying motive behind many of their hassles is to get their parents' attention or get their sibling into trouble.

Caroline sometimes bugs her siblings, especially her next older brother, Thomas. She plays the piano very loudly when he is doing his homework and refuses to stop, even though he

asks her politely. After a while Thomas loses his cool and shouts at his sister. When her brother shouts at her, Caroline begins whining or bursts into tears. At this point her mother comes into the room and reminds her that whining is not allowed. Caroline complains bitterly. "You always back up Thomas and you never back up me!"

Siblings who squabble within the family may become very protective of each other in other situations. Mark's older brother, Aaron, constantly tells Mark to be quiet and won't let him touch his video games. Yet, when Aaron is teased for wearing glasses, it is Mark who comes to his defense. Jeffrey and Ned, also close in age, have a similar relationship. Constantly competing at home, they cheer for each other on the soccer and baseball fields, and brag to their friends about each other's prowess.

When siblings are separated in age, the dynamics are different and conflicts are not as likely to occur. Xavier's mother talked about the warm and loving relationship between Xavier and his younger sister. Xavier tells his sister stories, reads her books, answers her questions, and kisses her every night before she goes to sleep. He loves to take on the role of teacher, explaining how to do things, teaching her the alphabet, and making up rules for games that she can understand. Kevin is especially protective of his younger sister, Carmen. He will sit by her side as she watches Barney, give her things she asks for, and play the games she chooses. Katie is infatuated with her teenage brother, Kenneth. She looks at him lovingly, jumps into his arms, and boasts to her friends that he is the tallest man in the whole wide world.

Although conflicts between siblings who are more than four years apart are less likely, they do occur. A likely cause is the younger child's pestering or interruption of the older one or resistance to the older child's control.

Lisa loves her two-year-old sister and gets along well with her most of the time. One day, however, she and her mother were playing with a floor puzzle. Her sister watched for a while and then reached down for a puzzle part and flung it across the room. Lisa was angry. "Why did she have to do that? That was mean," she told her mother. "Well," her mother answered, "she was just mad because we were playing and she felt left out." "Well then, why didn't she use her big girl words?" Lisa countered.

Justin reported the following altercation with his older brother, Elliott. "Elliott and I were having dinner with this really good popcorn shrimp—it's not really popcorn, it's tiny shrimp with this crusty stuff on it and it's really good—and I stole a popcorn shrimp from Elliott and he didn't even know and then I stole another one and we got into a fight. Then Mom said, 'Someone is going to get hurt,' so we stopped fighting."

Like Justin, Marvin loves to needle his older siblings. "He keeps bugging them until they get physical with him," reports his mother, "and then I intervene because I'm afraid he'll get hurt. Two seconds later, he needles again." Clearly, Marvin has his mother's number, and all the kids know it. They use it to their advantage when they want a treat from their parents. "Despite the fighting," his mother explains, "the siblings act as a team. If they want something, they have Marvin ask me if I'm in a good mood. If I say 'Yes,' Marvin makes the request."

PLAYING WITH ADULTS

Whether they are at home or at school, children between five and eight seek out opportunities to play with friends. For the most part the friends they select are peers, but children also love to play with adults, especially if the adults are their parents. In families where there is more than one child, most parents make a special effort to give each of their children private playtime. A common practice in many families is for parents to plan play days with each child on a regular basis.

When parents plan play days with their children, they are likely to choose activities that they themselves enjoy. Fathers are more likely than mothers to play ball, roughhouse, go fishing, or engage their child in an active sport. Mothers are more likely to play board games, do crafts, and go shopping with their children. Several parents used play days as a time to share their own special interests with their child.

The mother-daughter activities that Jenna's mother describes are fairly typical. They shop together, watch movies, read to each other, draw together, and write journals. Jenna's activities with her father are more unique. Jenna's father has two loves, electronics and popular music. Jenna and her father often play educational computer games and listen to music together. A favorite father-daughter activity is to pretend to be disc jockeys. Sometimes Jenna and her father take turns with a pretend microphone announcing the next selection. At other times they listen to new releases on the radio, give them a rating, and predict which selection is going to be the biggest hit.

As in Jenna's family, the father-son play in Mark's family reflects the special interests of his father. Mark's father is a scholar with special interest in ancient Egypt and Greece. He loves to read books to his son and takes great care to explain each illustration. When Mark went into the city with his father, his first request was to go and visit the tombstones.

Angela's mother loved arts and crafts and would always decorate T-shirts to sell at the school bazaar. Angela and her mother would go to the store together and buy neat things like feathers, beads, and sequins, which they would glue on to the T-shirts.

Although children's primary adult friends tend to be their mothers and fathers, many five-to-eight-year-olds develop strong ties to other adult friends. Becky had a close relationship with her grandfather, who lived on a farm in Virginia. When she visited him, they would collect chicken eggs from the barn and go out in the field to pick raspberries, which they would eat for dinner. One winter her mother gave her the choice of spending Christmas at home with her family so that they could open their Christmas gifts together, or going to Virginia to visit with her grandfather. "My Christmas gifts can wait," she told her mother. "I have to make Poppy Virginia happy. He's been sick."

Justin's best friend is the woman who lives next door. Nan has no children of her own and lives alone, but her house is almost always full of children. She keeps a stock of children's videos and video games, which she seems to enjoy as much as the kids do, and a large supply of games, toys, and stuffed animals. Nan frequently babysits for Justin, but to him, it is just another play date or pizza party.

Thomas lives part-time in Florida and part-time in New York. The very moment he arrives in Florida he runs next door to play with his neighbor, an avid gardener. Their special tie is their fascination with bugs or with anything that creeps or crawls. Together they collect worms, snails, newts, grasshoppers, frogs, lizards, chameleons, and spiders. One day Thomas caught a large cockroach in his bug catcher. Thomas showed his catch to his mother. "Look what I found, Mom. Isn't it interesting?"

ANSWERS TO PARENTS' QUESTIONS

My child doesn't talk about making friends at school. Should I speak with the teacher about it?

Feel free about talking with your child's teacher about your concern, but don't make an issue out of it. If the teacher tries too hard to force your child to make friends, it can be counterproductive. Certainly you want to be aware of your child's progress, but don't worry if she is slower to warm up than other children. Some children are "friends" with everyone; others value the intimacy of one or two close relationships, carefully chosen and deepened over time.

However, the teacher may have observed beginning or potential friendships that you could encourage. Perhaps there is another child in the class who is also shy or tends to be left out, or who shares a special interest of your child's. Perhaps there is a socially secure child who might smooth your child's entry into a group. The teacher could group or pair these children with your child for some activities; you could follow up by asking your child if she'd like to invite them to play. We have seen many cases where such a light "push" by teachers and parents resulted in deep and enduring friendships.

My child almost never invites children over to play unless I do the asking. Should I invite friends for him or should I wait for him to take the initiative?

Taking the initiative in inviting friends over is an important social skill. If you have a telephone with a memory dial, reserve two or three numbers for your child and give him the opportunity to punch in the numbers. Another way of encouraging your child to invite friends is to buy or make an appointment book. Let your child decide a week in advance whom he would like to invite to the house on a particular day. Put the phone number by his friend's name to avoid the usual excuse.

It is also a good idea to help your child plan a special activity that he can enjoy with a friend.

My son has a good friend who is a girl and the other children are beginning to tease him. How can I encourage my son to maintain this friendship?

Sometime between seven and ten years old, most children go through a period where they hate the opposite sex. It doesn't tend to last too long, particularly today when there are mixed sport teams. If the teasing bothers your son, he might spend less time with his girlfriend. At a later time the friendship is likely to be resumed.

My child likes to play with children who are younger than he is. Is this a cause for concern?

For the most part, it is good for children to spend time playing with both older and younger friends. For many children, younger friends provide an excuse for continuing imaginative play. It also gives them an opportunity to play both a leadership and a caregiving role. So long as your child does not behave on the level of the younger child, there is no cause for concern. If you do find, however, that your child is acting too "babyish," you may want to encourage him to join a sports group or interest club where there are children his own age.

My child is bereft because his best friend has developed other friendships and doesn't have much time for him. Although he will play with other children, he is not interested in making new friends.

Many parents of five-to-eight-year-old children have shared your concern. Provide opportunities for your child to make friends with a new child in a one-to-one situation. Invite a casual friend of your son's to go to the movies or a sports event with you. Give your child an opportunity to make friends with an adult or with a child who is either older or younger. As your child finds new friends to spend time with, he is less likely to miss the one best friend who is less interested in playing with him.

We have to move. Is there any way I could make the separation less painful for my child?

You are wise to think ahead about the impact on your child of leaving her friends. It will be important for her to maintain contact with her old friends and yet establish new ones. Before you leave the area, you might want to give your daughter's friends a gift of stamped postcards with your new address on them. Also prepare postcards for your own child with the addresses of her friends. If your daughter and her friends have access to e-mail, this is a splendid way to keep in touch.

Children between five and eight have many opportunities to make new friends that you need to capitalize on: neighborhood, school, church, organized clubs, sports teams, and other interest groups. Make sure that your child participates in the activities that are interesting to her. Invite children over to the house even if you haven't settled in. For the most part, children between five and eight are not likely to exclude a child because he or she is new to the neighborhood. A new child in town provides an opportunity for other children to enlarge their circle of friends.

Is it normal for children to fight with their friends?

There are very few children between five and eight years old who do not have disagreements with their friends. Children are likely to disagree about whose turn it is next, who gets a particular toy, who chooses the next activity, who gets to play the most desirable pretend role, who gets to sit in the most desirable seat, whose fault it was that something got broken, who won the game or who cheated. Other quarrels arise over hurt feelings. A child is possessive about friends and doesn't want them playing with anyone else. Someone is not invited to a party, or not asked to join a particular group. A child makes a disparaging remark about another child or calls another child names. Many of these quarrels are verbal, but others escalate into physical fights.

When should I intervene in a quarrel among friends?

Disagreements among friends may be disturbing to adults, but they are a potential learning experience for children. Resolving conflicts and negotiating compromises are important social skills that children develop in middle childhood. As long as children are able to settle their quarrels and reach an acceptable compromise without resorting to name calling or physical fights, parents should not be concerned when their child is involved in a disagreement.

When a conflict gets out of hand and you are afraid that someone will get hurt, it is natural to take action. It is also natural to take action when one child is being verbally abused by another child. The difficult decision is not whether to intervene but how to do it. Parents have several options: they can play the part of referee, they can suggest a cooling-off period, they can make a strong statement about no fighting, they can threaten to keep the children apart, or they can suggest a new activity that would be less likely to end up in a conflict. In most situations, it is best for parents to be calm and firm, making it clear that hurting each other is just not acceptable and giving children a new opportunity to reach a fair compromise.

My five-year-old's friendships are on-again and off-again. How should I handle it?

Many children at five years old are fickle about best friends. One day they may be bosom buddies with a child, and the next day they are archenemies. Quarrels between best friends are likely to occur for two reasons. First, like siblings, they know each other well, and can push just the right buttons when they want to annoy each other. Second, they feel safe fighting with a best friend because they know that rifts don't last very long. Just so long as your child is not upset by the rifts, it is best to ignore them. On the other hand, if your child is out of sorts or distraught, you may want to help her identify the source of the conflict, and brainstorm a way to reach a compromise with her friend without resorting to a rift.

My child can get awfully stubborn when she and her friends disagree. It's got to be her way or no way. How can I help her develop negotiating skills?

If your daughter is insistent about having her way, it is best to provide the opportunity for the peer group to initiate "corrective" answers. Quite often, the child who insists on being the director is valued by the peer group, who look to her as a leader. After a while, however, some members of the peer group are likely to become more assertive and your daughter will learn from experience that the peer group will not go along with her unless she is willing to compromise. When your daughter complains about their "attitude," it is time for you to help her learn about compromise and negotiation.

The most direct way to teach negotiation skills to a child is to talk about specific incidents that have occurred. If, for instance, your daughter wanted to play Nintendo and her friend wanted to play a board game, her friend may surprise her one day by saying, "I won't play Nintendo." Ask your daughter and her friend to think of different ways to solve the problem. Their list of solutions might include play Nintendo and then play a board game, play a board game and then play Nintendo, toss a coin to decide whether to play Nintendo, stop playing together, or choose a third activity that they both might enjoy. (You may want to offer suggestions.) Let the children decide which solutions would be fair and see if they can agree on one of the fair solutions. If you hold this same kind of conversation with your daughter on several occasions, she is likely to learn how to negotiate without your help.

What should I do if one child is left out of the play?

This situation requires some finesse. There are many reasons why the child may be left out; she may not like the activity that the others have chosen, she may be annoying or annoyed by the other children, or the others may be deliberately excluding her. If you insist on the children playing with the child who is being left out, you will make that child feel even more like a loser. If she seems distressed, it is usually better to involve the left-out child in a low-key activity, such as preparing a snack for the group, playing quietly with a puzzle or computer game, or reading a book. Sometimes, the exclusion is short-lived, and the child is included again as soon as the group moves on to a less-structured activity or one that is more to her liking. At a pause in the play, you might suggest a more inclusive activity, such as a snack or outdoor play, a game that requires three or more players, or a collective challenge like a scavenger hunt, building project, or baking activity. If exclusion and distress continue, it is best to send the visitors home as soon as you can.

When all the children have gone home, you can talk with your child about how she thinks the left-out child felt, and ask her to think up a way of making her feel included the next time the children come over.

Whenever possible, we advise having either two or more than three children, including close-in-age siblings, playing together. Three can be a setup for problems.

What should you do if your child and his friends have joined a clique where children talk about other children behind their backs or cruelly exclude them?

Joining a clique can be either positive or negative, depending on the values and activities of the clique members. In general, so long as a clique is not involved in dangerous, destructive, or aggressive activities, being a part of a clique can give children a feeling of being socially secure. It is important, however, to give your child opportunities to play with children who are not a part of the clique. If you feel that the clique your child has joined excludes other children in an unkind way, help your child take the point of view of the excluded child and let her find ways for the excluded child to gain admission to the group. Make sure that she and her friends recognize that cruel or negative remarks about other children are not appropriate and that even when they are said in private they are likely to get back to the child who is being maligned. Guard against making negative comments about your own friends or relatives within earshot of your child. Children are more likely to do what you do than to do what you say.

When your child is caught in a triangle with two children who both want to be his exclusive friend, what do you do?

Brainstorm a solution with your child. If he doesn't come up with a solution on his own, make some suggestions. Perhaps he can simply tell his two friends that he really likes them both and that all three friends should play together. Perhaps he would like to play with the two friends on alternative days, or perhaps he would like to invite a fourth child over so that they could avoid becoming a triangle. It may also be helpful to read a children's book such as *Leo, Zach and Emmy*, where the theme is a triangle friendship.

How should I handle it if my child is invited to a friend's house where the rules about watching X-rated or violent TV shows, or playing aggressive video games differ from the rules in our house?

It is always a difficult situation when friends come from homes that are very different in terms of prohibitions and limit setting. Telling your son that he cannot watch certain TV shows or play certain video games at his friend's house puts him in an untenable position. Either he has to disobey your rule, or risk rejection from his friend. Fortunately, unless a child has an aggressive personality to begin with, playing an aggressive video game is not going to change his personality, and watching an X-rated TV show is not going to make him precocious. Rather than facing the problem head-on, try some different tactics. Rent video games that are challenging but not violent, and videotapes that are clever or humorous but not X-rated. Encourage your son to invite his friends over to watch the videos or play the new video games. You might also talk to the friend's parents about your concerns. If you don't agree about particular games or shows, you might agree that the children should use their time together for outdoor activities, imaginative play, or creative projects rather than for playing video games or watching TV.

I am concerned about my son spending too much time watching TV or playing electronic games. What should I do about it?

Some parents set up rules for how much time their children are allowed to watch TV or play an electronic game. Other parents allow children to watch TV or play games as much as they like so long as they get their homework done. Still other families object to their children watching TV when they could be out playing active games. The American Academy of Pediatrics recommends that children watch no more than one to two hours of TV per day and that all programs they view be "developmentally based, prosocial, and nonviolent in nature."

How do I know if my child is socially on target?

Because social skills are critical for getting along in the world, all parents want to make certain that their child remains on target. It is easy to confuse social skills with personality differences. Some children are outgoing and make friends easily; other children are shy and make friends more slowly. A child who is shy and tentative in new social situations can be socially right on target. At the same time, a child who is socially outgoing may show signs of social immaturity. Here are some good indicators of good social adjustment:

- Enjoys playing with other children.
- Shows empathy when another child is hurt.
- Has at least one or two friends with whom he plays on a regular basis.
- Is not overly aggressive with other children.
- Is not usually selected as the victim.

PLAY IDEAS

- If your child has a new friend over and you are not certain about how it will work out, plan two or three activities that the children will enjoy, but do not introduce the activities if the children are doing fine on their own.
- It is quite common for a younger sibling to want to join the play when an older sibling has a friend over. Unless the older sibling wants his younger sibling to play, keep the younger sibling busy doing something with you. A good plan is to let the younger child help you to prepare a snack for the older children.
- If your child and a friend put on a play or a dance, help with props and costumes if and only if your child asks. Make sure to take time to watch their performance and applaud.
- Save craft materials such as egg cartons, paper towel or wrapping paper spindles, boxes of different sizes, scraps of gift paper, film canisters, buttons, fabric scraps, yarn, and string. Invite the children to make an original craft if your child is concerned about what to do with a friend.
- Encourage your child to play with a younger friend. Provide basic materials, like cars, toy animals, and play foods, that would encourage pretending. Older children are likely to enjoy the opportunity of directing imaginative play.

- Avoid triangle problems by introducing games that work best with three children, such as Life, Monopoly, or Clue, or by suggesting they put on a play.
- When children get into a hassle, give them an opportunity to solve it themselves. If they cannot resolve it, try replaying their hassle with two puppets (socks work well). Let the children resolve the conflict.
- Here is a simple game that can be used with a group of children who need help thinking of something to do or need to take time for a quiet, structured activity. Give each child three cards with the name of a friend on each card. The child whose turn it is describes something nice about the friend on her card. The other child or children try to guess whose name it is. If the first guess is right, she places the card on the table. If it is wrong, she gives the card to the child on her right. The game is over when all cards have been placed on the table.
- Play Scrabble cooperatively by encouraging players to help each other. The goal of the game is to see how high a combined score you can get. Let the children try to beat their own record.

- Play double solitaire cooperatively by seeing how many games you have to play before you both go out.
- Teach your child some games that you enjoyed when you were a child. He will enjoy teaching the games to a friend. Marbles, jump-rope rhymes, hopscotch, jacks, card games, dots, pick-up sticks, dominoes, Chinese checkers, clapping games, and cat's cradle are old favorites.
- Introduce your child to games that are played in different countries, such as mancala, mah-jongg, go, senet, and chess.
- Play games with your child to make car trips more fun:

COOPERATIVE GAMES

License plates: See how many out-of-state license plates you can count. Try to beat the record you set on a previous trip. You can also play a number game with license plates. Find a license with a #1, then search for a #2, etc. Set a goal of up to #10 on the first trip and continue to try to beat your record.

Alphabet game: Begin by finding a word on a sign beginning with an A. Continue going through the alphabet until you reach Z. Make an exception for X and Q. If you find them anywhere in a word, it counts.

Scavenger hunt: Before leaving home, make a list of things that you might find on your way. Give a copy of the list to each child. If you are driving in the country, you may want to include silo, barn, haystack, barbed-wire fence, railroad crossing, horse, cow, cat, dog, chicken, tractor, weathervane, wagon wheel. See how many of the items you can find.

COMPETITIVE GAMES

Geography: The first person names a place and the second person must name a place that begins with the last letter of the place's name; for example, the game might start out like this: New York, Kansas, San Francisco, Ontario, Ohio River. The same place cannot be used twice.

Ghost: In Ghost, players take turns adding one letter to make a word. The goal is not to be the one whose added letter completes a word of more than two letters. For example, the first person may say B, the next adds E, the third adds L. If the fourth person adds L or T, she makes a word and loses the round. If she adds C, she may force the next person to lose by adding H. If she adds a letter like J, the next person may challenge her to state the word she was trying to make. If it is misspelled or not a word, she loses the round. Each time a person loses a round, she gets one of the letters in "ghost." Whenever a person gets five letters (G-H-O-S-T), she is eliminated.

CHAPTER 4

Active Play

I'VE GOT WHEELS

Now that I can ride my bike
I can go anywhere I like.
I can even keep up on a long bike hike,
Cause I've got wheels!

On roller blades, I've got the knack
Of jumping over sidewalk cracks.
I can race to the store and be right back,
Cause I've got wheels!

The five-to-eight period is one of rapid physical development, when children gain new strength and new skills. Children who were awkward or uncoordinated in early childhood often become more coordinated and better able to keep up with peers. Children who had always seemed naturally athletic learn the controlled movements necessary for particular sports. Asked to name their children's favorite activities, most parents include several physical activities: skating or biking, one or more team sports; swimming, boating, hiking, or taking walks; dancing or gymnastics. Whether or not they engage in formal training or competitive sports, most five-to-eight-year-olds enjoy active play. Their play includes contact and cuddling, physical feats, being out and about, and participation in sports.

CONTACT AND CUDDLING

Among peers and siblings in the five-to-eight-year-old range, there is likely to be lots of touching. Pillow fights and wrestling matches; games of tackle, tag, and keep-away; and hand-clapping games all provide occasions for touching. In addition, it is not unusual to see friends walking down the halls at school holding hands, or with their arms around each other's shoulders. However, some children shy away from contact and may interpret even a minor shove as an aggressive act.

"Annie and Julie's favorite game is fighting," eight-year-old Callie reports after spending a day with her six- and eight-year-old cousins. "I couldn't get them to play with dolls or anything. They just wanted to get in fights and start laughing."

What Callie, a sensitive child whose only sibling is a very gentle thirteen-year-old brother, perceived as fighting, her cousins saw as fun. Well-coordinated, active, and adept at gymnastics, they enjoyed wrestling, roughhousing, and tickling, especially with each other.

Sometimes, the contact games take the form of teasing:

tickling or threatening to tickle, poking, touching surreptitiously and running away, chasing to catch or tackle, or hat stealing. This physical teasing is especially common in cross-gender play, and boys or girls often egg each other on in games of get-the-girls, chase-the-boys, or don't-catch-the-cooties. In some groups, one child is repeatedly chosen as the messenger to initiate this kind of play. For example, Xavier is often elected as the one to bother the girls because he is willing to go along with the group's requests and because the other children consider him "handsome."

Though some boys develop a distinct aversion to kissing, most five-to-eight-year-olds like to be hugged and cuddled, especially by their parents. They will snuggle in bed, sit on laps

for reading or watching TV, roll on the floor and wrestle, enjoy a tickle fest, jump eagerly into waiting arms, request a goodnight kiss or backrub before going to sleep, and, when they are lucky enough to be light or to have strong parents, take piggyback or shoulder rides whenever they can get them. Seven-and-eight-year-olds who decide they are too big to cuddle with their parents in bed may enjoy giving them back rubs or foot massages. Many parents are pleasantly surprised that their children continue to enjoy cuddling and hugging beyond their preschool years.

PHYSICAL FEATS

"Look at me!" yells eight-year-old Julie, as she effortlessly turns a handspring. "Hey, Mark. Can you do this?" Her six-year-old cousin attempts a cartwheel, managing to keep his feet off the ground, though his legs are not straight. For the next half hour,

the children take turns displaying their tricks, occasionally reminding the adults to pay attention and cheer.

While not all five-to-eight-year-olds can turn cartwheels,
most develop a repertoire of tricks—standing on their hands in
a swimming pool, jumping over a couch, turning somersaults,
working a yo-yo or hula hoop, demonstrating karate moves.

For five-year-old Alice, physical prowess is her growing edge. She is constantly exploring what she can do with her body. How high a ledge can she jump from? How long can she balance on her hands? Can she jump into the air and spin all the way around? Can she leap and twirl like the ballet dancers in *The Nutcracker*? Can she dance like a rock star?

Eight-year-old Marissa is also constantly in motion. When she's not practicing gymnastics or doing tricks on the backyard swing, she's jumping over furniture and trying to climb up walls. Having started gymnastics classes at five, she now spends eight to ten hours a week in formal practices and meets. Yet she always seems ready for more. For Marissa, who likes to read and draw and play card games but is less interested in pretending or in playing with toys, physical play is the most fun kind.

Six-year-old Jessica, who is not generally very physical, loves it when her eight-year-old neighbor, Randy, comes over. Randy suggests new games, like chasing after monsters or jumping off the couch into the "ocean," which Jessica later extends with her younger sister.

OUT AND ABOUT

Most five-year-olds are kept under close adult supervision, but, depending on the neighborhood and their parents' level of trust, sometime between six and eight, children begin to go places on their own. At first, it may only be running ahead on a family walk and stopping at the corners, but soon children want to visit neighbors, play in the yard or park without supervision, cross streets by themselves, walk to the corner store or bus stop with an older friend or sibling, and ride their bikes around the neighborhood or to and from school.

Katie, at six, loves to go on adventures and is usually quite a daredevil. When her family went skiing in Colorado, Katie raced her parents down the steepest runs. When she went to

Disney World for the weekend, she begged her sister to take her to Space Mountain, a ride that her mother much preferred not to go on. When Katie visited her mother in the office, however, she would not go across the hall to the bathroom unless her mother accompanied her.

In contrast to Katie, Justin has no fears about going outside on his own. He has finally gotten his parents to allow him to visit neighbors, as long as he says where he is going and has an older person watching when he crosses the street. The moment he gets home from school, Justin is out and about, looking for someone to play with.

Having the run of the backyard or the neighborhood is especially appealing when there are lots of kids around to play with, so that play dates don't have to be arranged. Looking out the window, Bobby sees neighborhood kids riding bikes or tossing a ball, and rushes out to join them. Games of catch or tag are easy to expand to include other players. Hide and Seek is a favorite, even more fun outdoors where you can run freely than it is in a house full of good hiding places.

Riding a two-wheeler or getting around on roller skates, Roller Blades, or a skateboard is in many ways like learning to walk—it gives you a whole new status and perspective. For some kids, bike riding comes easy. They straddle the bike, push off with their feet, and glide along. After coasting short distances, they get up the nerve to try the pedals. Persistent in their efforts or naturally balanced and unafraid, they learn to ride in a short time.

For other kids, learning to ride a bike is work, and they often have scrapes and bruises to prove it. Jeffrey became increasingly frustrated as he watched his friend Arran struggle and finally master the art of bike riding. "Now I'm the only eight-year-old in the world who can't ride a bike," Jeffrey grumbled, refusing to let Arran's father or anyone else help him learn. Fortunately, Jeffrey had become adept on Roller Blades before Arran mastered them. Playing together, the boys were able to coach and goad each other as they spent hour after hour going up and down their dead-end street. By the end of the summer, they were on top of the world—able to take long bike rides with their parents and play Roller Blade street hockey with each other.

For Sonia, whose big sister Marissa was a natural-born athlete, learning to skate was a chore to be endured. Her mother decided lessons would help, and took Sonia to a rink. At first, Sonia seemed to spend most of the time sitting down. Every time she fell, she sat quietly until someone came to pull her up. After the lesson, Sonia described what had happened. "My invisible friends, Jimmy and Kerry, were trying to learn, too. Jimmy couldn't do it at all. He kept falling down and I had

to tell him that it was okay, he'd get it if he kept trying. But Kerry was really good. Did you see her racing around the rink?" After a few more lessons, Sonia noticed that all three of them— Kerry, herself, and even Jimmy—were very good skaters.

Ethan's experience was similar. A very verbal and naturally cautious child, he is always reluctant to try a new physical activity. His reaction to swimming, ice skating, and Roller Blading was the same: initial reluctance, fear of failure, and fear of getting hurt. Yet in each case Ethan's love of learning new things led to a fascination with the procedures and tricks of the trade. Following the instructions carefully, he was able to master each new skill.

Learning to ride a bike, having the stamina for a long hike or mountain climb, or being able to catch a baseball open up new possibilities for family play. Christopher loves to ride bikes in the park with his father, or toss a baseball back and forth. James likes to challenge his mother to a basketball game. Alice and her dad go kayaking when they want special time together.

Clubhouses, forts, and secret hideouts are popular gathering spots in neighborhoods with lots of kids. In Justin's neighborhood, the kids like to hang out in the backyard with a treehouse. James and his buddies like to play in a special spot by the lake. Jake's backyard contains an old rowboat, which sets the stage for all kinds of fantasy play. Ned and his friends are always building backyard forts, though they sometimes have trouble getting them to stay up. Collecting food, flashlights, and other camping stuff, they pretend to go on rugged adventures where they must survive on their own.

For some children, gardens have special appeal. Bobby loves to pick the grapefruit from his tree and "sell" it to his family and neighbors. Alice likes to take her rocking chair outside so she can sit and watch her roses grow. Benjamin likes to dig in the dirt, and gets especially excited when he finds a worm. Jessica loves to pretend that she could live in her garden. She munches on mint, oregano, tomatoes, and berries; picks catnip for the neighbor's cat, and imagines the two of them living in the fort on the top of her swing set. For Arran and Myles, a couple of boards and the corner of a fence are enough to make a fort, and a patch of dirt sparks all sorts of imaginative play. One day, the boys buried toys and chicken bones, hoping they would turn into fossils.

Nature walks are always fascinating. In an urban area, children can find squirrels and birds, bugs hiding under rocks, flowers growing out of sidewalk cracks, hidden gardens, and many kinds of street trees and shrubbery. If they know where to look, children may even find edible fruit, places where animals

could nest, anthills, soft carpets of moss, and slimy slugs. In suburban and rural areas there may be streams where they can catch minnows, frogs, or crayfish; secret hideouts between rocks or behind fallen trees; trees that can be climbed; animal holes, droppings, or tracks to discover.

Many children like to collect natural objects—rocks, shells, unusual seed pods, fall leaves, flowers, or acorns. They may keep them in special boxes or "treasure cans," display them on shelves, or combine them with small toys and objects for use in imaginative play, art projects, or building. Alice, whose family is Buddhist, likes to collect offerings of natural objects to place before the statue of Buddha or in other special places around the house. Brittany likes to make "concoctions," "potions," and pretend food with the leaves, twigs, and seeds she collects, mixing them with dirt and water. Her collections of rocks and acorns are prized, kept in secret drawers, and played within the privacy of her bedroom. Thomas, an inveterate collector, was thrilled to find a fossil bone that he could not identify. He pleaded with his father to take him to the local science museum, convinced that he had a valuable treasure. He wasn't far wrong; the fossil he picked up on the beach turned out to be from the "femur of a whale not usually found in northern waters."

Justin and his big brother Elliott keep family nature hikes interesting by bringing along their toy guns. They race ahead, hide

behind trees and bushes, and play endless games of chase and ambush. Justin is just as happy, though, to carry a bag and collect exotic objects that he finds along the trail.

Of course, nothing beats a real excursion: a family camping trip, a canoe ride down a river, or a visit to an exotic locale. For James and his family, summer vacations are an opportunity for adventure. When James was five years old, he and his family went to New Harbor, Maine, and stayed in a small unfinished cabin. As always, the vacation was unstructured and James was in charge of creating his own fun. James loved going down to the harbor to watch the fishermen lift anchor in the morning and come back at sundown to unload their catch. He also loved to run around town and visit the boat-building places. His favorite pastime, however, was going down to the shore, digging up mussels, and panning for "gold." When it was time to fly

home, despite his family's mild protestations, James carried a large bucket of rocks on board the plane. This was his treasure collection, and he spent many hours arranging and rearranging his "golden nuggets." "I'm not ready for going home," James protested at the end of the vacation.

At six years old, James went with his family to Cape Cod. The ocean was too cold to swim in, but James had a wonderful time exploring the salt marshes, skipping stones in a nearby pond, and boarding old restored ships.

When James was seven, he and his family went to North Carolina. They camped out, putting up a tent, sleeping in sleeping bags, gathering firewood, and cooking their food over an open fire. Often the pancakes came out flat and the potatoes turned to charcoal, but nobody, least of all James, was bothered. During the day the family hiked up the Appalachian trail, hunted for hidden waterfalls, and slid down boulders. After dinner, when it was turning dark, they gathered their flashlights, slipped into their sleeping bags and read themselves to sleep. At the end of the vacation James boarded the plane with a giant-size walking stick.

The next summer, when James was eight, the family went back to North Carolina. They rented an old house, which belonged to a man who ran a general store and which had been

preserved by the historic society. During the day James and his family went tubing and white-water rafting. In the middle of the vacation, an old friend came to visit. For the first time in his life James got to shoot a real gun. "We didn't shoot anything living," he assured his mother. "We were only practicing." In the evening, when everyone else was exhausted, James insisted on going for a walk. He chased and caught butterflies, releasing them immediately and watching them fly away. Like the butterflies, James was liberated by his summer vacations.

SPORTS

"Batter up!" the umpire calls, and eight-year-old Jennifer steps up to the plate. "Strike her out!" a parent yells from the stands, and the opposing team begins a rapid chant of "batter-batter-batter-batter" designed to distract Jennifer. Concentrating as hard as she can, Jennifer watches as the pitch is thrown. "Ram

it down her throat!" calls one of her teammates, and Jennifer swings with all her might. "Strike one." "I should have had that," mumbles Jennifer, annoyed with herself, as she determinedly sets up for the next pitch.

Many children—and many parents—are uncomfortable with this level of pressure and competitiveness and feel that it takes the fun out of the game. Yet some children thrive on discipline and competition, driving themselves to excel.

For Nicky, a shy child who worked hard to do well in school, baseball became an obsession. Nicky watched it on TV whenever he could, studying the players' movements and strategies. He rented videos to learn batting, fielding, and pitching techniques, and practiced them over and over by himself or with his father. When he began to read chapter books, he chose only baseball stories and biographies. When asked to write a story or create a math problem, he always found a way to involve baseball. He became an expert on baseball trivia and statistics, and an avid collector of baseball cards. As his prowess on the field and knowledge of the game increased, so did his social and academic confidence. Having learned to perform in crunch situations on the field, he was less afraid of new experiences.

Most five-to-eight-year-olds enjoy less competitive sports programs, where emphasis is on having fun and learning skills. Rules may be modified so that everyone feels successful. For example, practice T-Ball games can be played so that outs are called but runners remain on base and continue to play until they get home. Clever coaches turn drills into chase-the-coach games, obstacle courses, and relay races, keeping the pace quick and the pressure light. In some programs the ethic is one of support and teamwork. Children are expected to cooperate with their teammates, try their best, and make supportive comments in the face of both success and failure. They are discouraged from saying anything negative to or about the other team, and may even compliment an opposing player on an especially good play. At the end of the game, opposing teams may give cheers for each other, shake hands, and congratulate each other on a "good game."

Yet, even within this less competitive ethos, many children are intensely competitive. Ned, at seven, is an experienced and intense soccer player, with an overwhelming desire to win. He goes along with the rules against making disparaging comments, but competes as intensely as he can. Although he is a compassionate child who never hesitates to give deserved credit—even to a rival—he will do whatever is necessary to win a game. If he misses a goal or is outmaneuvered by an opposing player, he will get down on himself and sulk for hours. If someone suggests that he is not the best player on the team, he is likely to get angry. Pickup games with his brother and his brother's friends sometimes end in physical fights, especially when Ned is put in the frustrating position of not having a chance to win. Ned's interest in soccer is so intense that he will even watch a professional game that is broadcast in Spanish if he can't find it on an English-language channel.

Steven, an equally athletic and sports-minded seven-year-old, is just becoming interested in soccer. Before he commits to playing this new sport, he wants to spend some time practicing with peers and watching others play. He needs to size up the situation, to make sure that he will be good enough. He doesn't need to be the best, but he wants to make sure that he won't be embarrassed.

Many five-to-eight-year-olds, especially boys, fancy themselves professional ball players and spend endless hours tossing a ball and catching it in a baseball glove, shooting baskets, or

kicking goals. They frequently accompany their play with a sportscaster's play-by-play monologue, putting themselves in the hero role. "Here we are folks. The seventh game of the World Series, three balls, two strikes, two outs, the Red Sox are winning by one. Here's the pitch. It's a long fly ball to deep center field. It's going, going . . . caught by Bardige, an amazing catch! The Red Sox have won the World Series!"

ANSWERS TO PARENTS' QUESTIONS

My child wants to be more independent—to play in the park without me watching, to go to her friend's house by herself, to ride her bike to the corner store. I don't want to discourage her, but I have some concerns about safety. At what age is she old enough to go places on her own? How can I help her be safe without making her inappropriately fearful?

Your concerns are understandable. Choosing between encouraging independence and keeping a child safe can be a hard call. Because the safety of your neighborhood and the trustworthiness of your child are part of the equation, it is difficult to determine at what age your child should go places on her own. Decide which places you would feel most comfortable about having her go and think about what concerns you might have if she went to these places. If you are worried about her crossing the street or talking to strangers, teach her safety rules before you grant permission. Try a practice run with your child to a selected destination. Stay just far enough behind so that she feels independent but you could get to her in an emergency. Once she has learned the rules, continue to expand her privileges so long as she proves to be trustworthy.

My child isn't interested in sports yet. What should I do to encourage her?

If your child isn't interested in sports, the first question you need to ask yourself is "why?" Is she focused on other activities that take up her free time? Has she had a bad experience, such as falling off a bicycle or getting hit by a baseball, that makes her shy away from sports? Are her close friends interested in sports? Has she had an opportunity to try different types of sports?

Participating in sports is important for children, but this does not mean that all children need to join Little League or play on a soccer team. Some children shy away from group or contact sports and prefer individual or partner sports like bike riding, martial arts, gymnastics, dance, Frisbee, jump rope, horseback riding, bowling, skating, rock climbing, fishing, boating, hiking, or swimming. Provide your child with an opportunity to try out a variety of sports. As soon as you find physical activities that she really enjoys, encourage her to continue. Help her find friends who share her burgeoning interest. If you or your spouse has a particular interest in a sport that does not appeal to your child, be careful not to overemphasize the importance of that sport.

Is it as important for girls as it is for boys to participate in sports?

Although physical prowess is more likely to be the basis for popularity with boys than it is with girls, physical activities are important for all children. With some exceptions based on physique, girls today are not only participating in team sports with the same intensity as boys, they are also joining sport teams that were once exclusively male. It is equally true that boys are participating more and more in activities that were once considered to belong exclusively to girls. Tap, ballet, and ballroom dancing are significant examples. Research shows that sports may be even more important for girls than for boys; girls who participate in sports as children and teenagers are likely to feel better about themselves, do better in school, and be healthier as adults than girls who don't.

In my town, competitive sports start at five. Is this too young? Will my child be able to catch up if he starts at eight or nine?

Children who start a year or two later than their peers may be at a temporary disadvantage, but they catch up quickly if they are well coordinated and enjoy the sport.

If your child is interested in participating in a team sport at a young age, select a team or class that is not overly competitive or demanding. The decision of when and if to enlist your child in a more competitive and demanding sport or team should be made on the basis of your child's temperament and interests. Some children enjoy a competitive and disciplined team when they are as young as six years old. Other children may not be ready until they are older. Still other children may never be ready. Take your cue from your child.

PLAY IDEAS

- Children enjoy learning old-fashioned games and tricks, especially when they have been handed down through generations and come with family stories. Introduce your child to games you enjoyed as a child, such as Chinese jump rope, hopscotch, limbo, hand clapping, jump-rope rhymes, and ball-bouncing games like A, My Name Is Alice. Teach your child some tricks you mastered, such as whistling with a blade of grass, working a yo-yo or bolo bat, or walking around with a book on your head or a spoon on your nose.
- Filled with different substances, balloons make simple toys that encourage active play. Fill balloons with water, and let children throw them at targets, play Keep Away or Monkey in the Middle, or see how many times they can toss the balloons back and forth before dropping or popping them. Encourage children to invent their own rules for cooperative and competitive games with air-filled or water-filled balloons. Using a funnel, fill balloons with sand, flour, or cornmeal to make balls that are fun to squeeze, juggle, and catch.
- Make an obstacle course for your child; then encourage her to vary it by herself or with a friend. You can use large pillows, outgrown preschool climbing structures, jump ropes, hula hoops, towels, mats, low tables that can be crawled under, or outdoor items such as swings, tires, lad-

ders, and balance boards. Children will enjoy making up the rules for the course, including what must be gone over, under, through, or around in what order. If you have appropriate outdoor space, children can also make courses for bikes or roller skates.

• Whether it is for an afternoon, an overnight, or a week, camping out is a special treat for most five-to-eight-year-olds. The location does not need to be exotic; a porch, a backyard tent, a rooftop deck, even a homemade fort can be a fascinating place to listen to a bedtime story, share a special snack, or spend the night. The fun can be enhanced by taking a long "hike" or "flashlight walk" to the destination, even if you end up where you began.

• A shallow stream can provide endless hours of fun as children balance on rocks; try to jump across; build log bridges; float paper boats; investigate what lies under the rocks; look for fish, tadpoles, and bugs; create dams; track seasonal changes in water depth; break the winter ice; or just mess around in the mud and water.

• When you go on nature walks or hikes with your child, bring along some plastic bags for carrying home treasures. Searching for unusual seedpods, pebbles, shells, berries, leaves, or other small objects can make the walk more fun. Depending on your child's interests, she may want to identify her finds, use them in a collage or other art project, or add them to a collection.

• Almost every errand can be turned into an adventure. A trip to the grocery store can become a hunt for ingredients for a special dinner, with an item from each continent or a favorite food for each person in the family. A set of boring errands can become a special together time if you can plan together with your child so that boring stops are preludes to simple treats, like cutting through the park or buying ice cream.

- I Spy hunts are fun for same-age or mixed-age groups. Make a list of things to look for. Your list can include specific items, like a pine cone or a Japanese maple leaf; general categories like an animal's home, an unripe fruit, a plant with thorns, or a flower that attracts bees or butterflies; hard-to-find objects like a pink car or a four-leaf clover; transient phenomena like a dried-up puddle or an anthill; or special places like a house with a hexagonal window, a fire hydrant, or a birdbath. Children check off items when they are seen. Send the children out in one or more groups, and set boundaries and safety rules before they go. The fun is in the finding, not the competition, so it is okay to have only one group. For younger children, you might have them help you draw up the list of things to look for and then accompany them on the search.
- A scavenger hunt, where children collect the objects on a list, is an easy outdoor activity that can be played by groups of two or more children, working together or on competing teams. To set up the hunt in advance, place simple items like pennies, paper clips, rubber animals, bolts, clothespins, etc. on the steps or around the house. Alternatively, you can make a list of items that children are likely to find. Here are some examples:

  - an oak leaf
  - a pink flower petal
  - a rock with a stripe on it
  - a ball
  - a piece of bark
  - a leaf that is not green
  - a bug
  - an envelope
  - a gum or candy wrapper
  - a seed
  - something you can write with

• Treasure hunts are very popular with five-to-eight-year-olds. Their new ability to read, combined with an emerging ability to interpret puns and double meanings, makes treasure hunts both fun and challenging. Here is an example of an "outside-the-house" treasure hunt:

Use different-colored index cards for each team. On one side of the index card put the clue number. On the back side of the index card write a simple verse that leads the children to the next clue. Use the same clues for each team, but arrange them in a different order.

Clue # 1. If you stare at a back porch stair, you'll find the next clue hiding there.

Clue # 2. Where's the next clue? Where could it be? Look in the shade of an old apple tree.

Clue # 3. If it's starting to rain and it's too wet outside, find the next clue in a good place to hide.

Clue # 4. It's easy to find the very next clue. There could be a letter in there for you.

Clue # 5. The next clue you'll find is most likely hid, in a good place for jumping, if you're a kid.

Clue # 6. If you pump hard on this you will think you can fly. The clue's under its seat, not way up in the sky.

Clue # 7. (The last clue for both teams.) You've found all the clues. You've done very well. I'll give you the treasure when you ring the bell.

• Arrange family or neighborhood ball games in which adults and children of different ages play on the same team. Modify the rules if necessary to give the youngest players a chance to score. With mixed ages and genders, the competition tends to be less and the fun enhanced!

• You can help your child learn sports skills by playing simple games. Stand close together and toss a baseball back and forth. Each time someone catches it, take a small step backward. Each time someone drops it, take a small step forward. Set up targets to hit by throwing or kicking. Create obstacle courses for dribbling, using sandbags, outdoor furniture, or chalk markings.

• For serious sports players, how-to videos can be helpful learning tools. For example, you might find a video that teaches batting techniques. You and your child can watch it together; then you can help her practice. Some cities also offer week-long summer and school vacation "camps" in which young players can improve their skills.

• Get a book on "new" or "noncompetitive" games and learn ways to vary old standbys like Duck, Duck, Goose; dodge ball; and musical chairs, so that children don't get "out" and have to wait a long time before they can play again. Learn cooperative games like Sticky Popcorn, in which children jump around like popcorn kernels and "stick" to anyone they bump into. The cooperative *Sports and Games Book* is a classic.

CHAPTER 5

Creative Play

When I grow up, I want to be a thilantrokist.
I will have lots of clothes and toys and candy
and good food and I will give people whatever
they need. —ALICE, AGE 5

Creativity is a hallmark of children five to eight. Children are not only creative in their thinking, but they are also able to create original products, drawings, crafts, songs, stories, and poems. At five and six years old, there is a joyfulness in children's creative work. The exuberance and imagination of their products makes up for their deficiences in form, precision, and detail. The crafts may be flimsy, the songs tuneless, the stories disconnected, or the jokes pointless, but their creators are enamored with the process and happy with the end product.

With seven- and eight-year-olds, we see a different picture. Although children remain creative, they are more self-conscious about their products and keep working at a project until they get it right. Seven- and eight-year-olds are also adept at recognizing their own talents. If they feel they are good storytellers, they will invest their energy in writing stories. If they feel they are good artists, they will spend endless hours perfecting their drawing or sculpture. Some children specialize even further. Jeannie discovered that she was quite good at drawing rabbits. Week after week and month after month the only thing Jeannie drew were rabbits, which became more stylized with each rendition.

In this chapter we will look both at children's creative play and their creative products. We focus on music, art, crafts, building, cooking, and storytelling, jokes, and spoofs. Dance and drama are discussed in the next chapter on Pretend Play.

MUSIC

"Turn off that tape," Sarah insisted as she drove to school with her mother. "Rafi is for babies, and I am five years old." Like Sarah, five-year-olds are likely to quite suddenly decide that some music is for babies, and they don't want to listen to it. Just as carrying a Barney towel can peg you as a baby, so can listening to music written for preschoolers. These reactions to music, of course, have more to do with the peer culture than the actual appeal of the music.

At the same time that children are rejecting "baby" music, they are becoming more invested in putting on musical performances. Five-year-olds love to sing. Whether or not they can carry a tune, most five-year-olds welcome the opportunity to put on a solo performance or sing along with a group. This love of singing is unlikely to diminish as children get older, but as they grow older children become increasingly more self-critical. Unless they are sure that they have a good voice, they are embarrassed about singing solo in front of an audience.

Often children get silly when they sing. As long as they are acting silly, nobody will tell them that they can't carry a tune. It is also quite safe to be a part of a sing-along, where nobody really cares how well you sing as long as you sing nice and loud. Phoebe came home after her Brownie meeting and told her mother that she had learned two new Girl Scout songs. "Well sing them to me," her mother requested. "No, I can't," Phoebe explained, "you are only supposed to sing them with lots of other people."

At six years old some children begin to take formal music lessons. They start off with enthusiasm, but, whether or not they have talent, practicing is likely to be a battle. Inevitably, parents find themselves in a dilemma. "If he doesn't practice I'm wasting my money and should probably let him quit. If I let him quit, however, he'll never get good enough to really enjoy it and besides he might get the idea that it's okay to start lessons and then quit as soon as it gets hard."

Tracy's mother solved the "won't practice" dilemma by telling Tracy that it was time to take a piano recess. They would start again next year. Danny's mother agreed to sit with him at the piano if he promised to practice for fifteen minutes. In actuality, the basic problem is that many children begin formal lessons too early. It's fun for a short time, but then the practicing gets tedious. Unfortunately most children are not cut out to be a Mozart. It's better to encourage young children to appreciate music than to try to turn them into serious musicians before they are really ready.

Beginning around six and seven years old, children develop a taste for the popular music of the day. Listening to music becomes a social activity. Friends get together, turn on a CD, and dance or sing with the music. Ned and his friends, at seven years old, not only had developed a taste for rap music, but could recognize songs and artists after just a few words.

For some children, music is not just a way of having fun; it is an important part of their lives. Danny has loved listening to music since he was an infant. At four years old a favorite activity was going to concerts with his mother. At five years old, he was obsessed with sound-making instruments. He would blow into harmonicas, kazoos, shofars, and soda bottles and was delighted with himself when he could make notes come out. At six he was taking piano, violin, and drum lessons, making up lyrics, and humming and singing whenever there was downtime.

From the point of view of Danny's classroom teacher, there was a downside to Danny's nonstop singing. Danny not only sang popular songs but often rewrote the lyrics to songs to make them silly or gross. One day Danny's mother got a telephone call from the school suggesting that she and his teacher have a serious talk. During the serious talk Danny's mother was told that her son had destroyed the decorum of the hallways. He had rewritten the words to "Take Me Out to the Ball Game" and taught them to his classmates. On the way from the lunchroom to the classroom, with Danny in the lead, all the children sang:

> *Take me out to the hospital.*
> *Take me out to my room.*
> *Buy me some Band-Aids and water, too.*
> *I don't care if I throw up on you.*
> *For it's root, root, root for the hospital.*
> *If I don't die, it's a shame.*
> *For it's eat, drink, barf in the sink*
> *At the old hospital!*

ART

The drawings of the five-year-old are fun to look at. Megan's picture of a girl standing under a rainbow with rain falling all around her is typical of a five-year-olds drawings. It has balance and movement and the raindrops sprinkled around the rainbow give it a fanciful feeling. It doesn't matter whether Megan's girl is standing at an angle, or if her hair comes down to her legs, or if one hand has three fingers. Megan is not trying to draw an exact picture of a child standing under a rainbow. She has put together some of the elements she knows how to draw in a way that is pleasing to her.

Six-year-old Kevin, like Megan, has filled his paper with forms he has mastered—grass, clouds, birds, a rainbow, a house with windows and a door, and two stick figures. He has also added three figures that are harder to identify. The largest of the figures may be an overgrown butterfly, and a second figure

very well may be a bird. The most fascinating part of the picture is that the figures he has labeled Kevin and Mommy are standing together holding hands inside an enclosure that separates them from the house, the animals, and even the rainbow. We could interpret Kevin's picture as a wish fulfillment. What could be better than standing in a safe place hand in hand with your mother in the center of a busy universe.

Steven, who is also six years old, has unusual artistic ability. His Halloween scene is full of scary things: a bat is flying overhead, alligators are swimming in the water that flows under a drawbridge, a ghost is flying in the sky, and a tombstone is placed on each side of the drawbridge. Steven's drawing is beautifully executed, revealing the promise of an artist in the making.

Drawing is a favorite activity of five- and six-year-olds. Five-year-olds are likely to create designs, rainbows, families, houses, and flowers. Six-year-olds are likely to draw landscapes with ground lines, skies, trees, flowers, and grass or to create vehicles going along a road or a track.

Seven- and eight-year-olds are likely to be more critical about their drawing skills than five- and six-year-olds. If they feel that they are not good artists, they may stop drawing altogether or draw only stylized cartoon figures or other pictures that they can copy. Children who have more confidence in their artistic ability may work hard at improving their drawing. They pay attention to placement and proportions and are unlikely to draw a figure taller than a house or floating around in space. They also pay attention to detail and are concerned with accuracy and precision. It is not unusual for seven- and eight-year-olds to figure out how to draw a particular object like an airplane, race car, horse, cartoon hero, or rabbit and to continue to draw the same object over and over again, adding new details and improving their composition.

Jeannie had a special aptitude for drawing rabbits. She began drawing rabbits when she was five years old, and at seven her fascination with the subject had not diminished. Jeannie was somewhat scrawny at five, but by seven years she had rounded out and, as you can see by the picture, so had her rabbit.

Jenna, like her brother Steven, was a talented artist. Always a perfectionist, she spent a long time working on each of her drawings and was never satisfied until every detail was in place. Her drawing of an arrangement of jack-o'-lanterns was true to life and nicely composed, and incorporated several jokes that she had learned.

For children like Jeannie and Steven, drawing is a private activity, an opportunity to express ideas or create a self-satisfying drawing. For other children, drawing is a social activity. Young children love to copy from each other and are pleased rather than offended when another child copies their ideas. When José got the idea of putting a face on his sun and sunglasses on the sun's nose, a whole row of children produced sunny-day drawings with big smiling suns sporting sunglasses.

Many seven- and eight-year-olds who are not confident about their drawing skills love to draw with another child. These joint drawings very often turn out to be a kind of pretending. Ned and Sam decided to draw a page full of weird figures.

They competed with each other to see who could draw the stupidest-looking guy. The two boys talked nonstop as they drew preposterous pictures of guys with four arms, hair standing up like wire, oversized eyeballs, and fangs. Siri and Elena found a different way of drawing together. They made up a story about two hungry skeletons that went on an eating binge. As they told the story, they took turns drawing "yucky" foods: a hairy lollipop, a hot dog covered with muck, and a plateful of worms.

Becky, who really loved to draw but was not very good at it, decided to make a comic strip. She began by drawing two stick figures with round heads and speech bubbles coming out of their mouths. In the first speech bubble she wrote, "Want to go on a date?" In the second bubble she wrote, "A date with you? Ha ha ha!" Her friend, Sarah, who also had trouble with free drawing, spent hours copying the pilgrims and cornucopias on a Thanksgiving napkin.

CRAFTS

Crafts were mentioned as a favorite activity by many of the parents. The appeal of making a craft for some of the children was the sensation of feeling gooey, viscous materials and the fun of making a mess. Alice enjoyed making clay with her own flour-and-water recipe. It didn't matter at all whether it could be shaped; the fun was in the mixing.

Several children were concerned with the end product and enjoyed working with store-bought craft kits. Caroline made bead jewelry, Myles glued together model cars, Marissa made lanyards and key chains from gimp, Becky punched out Play Doh cookies and served them to her mother's guests. James started with an origami kit but preferred to do it his own way. One night he stayed up until two in the morning making a fleet of paper airplanes.

For the most part, children steered away from packaged craft material. They enjoyed the challenge of making collages out of materials they found in the yard or around the house, decorating shoe boxes, and making paper-doll clothes from scraps of paper. Most of all, however, children liked making things that they could incorporate into their imaginative play. Jennifer painted blocks so that they looked like stores, houses, or buildings, and used them as part of a Disney World theme park. Sonia and Marissa layered sand in long-necked bottles and glued on funny faces to make a circus troupe. James turned a large lump of clay into a family of monkeys. Ned made rockets and spaceships from milk cartons.

Jessica made a paper castle by taping sheets of paper together to form a cube, cutting out small window slits on the sides and leaving a large opening for the front door. Next, she cut a strip of paper and attached one end to the front of the castle in an apparent attempt to make a drawbridge. Finally, she cut out a paper king and attached him with string to the inside of the castle. She was enormously proud of her product and told herself a story as she moved the king in and out.

BUILDING

Building is a favorite activity for many five-to-eight-year-olds, both boys and girls. They love to design elaborate structures, vehicles, and scenes from blocks or from snap-together materials like Legos or Connex. Most five-to-eight-year-old builders tend to specialize—they become experts at using a particular kind of toy to build a particular kind of model. David and Paul like to build with Connex—short sticks connected by multi-pronged fasteners. They've made a wide array of miniature play structures—merry-go-rounds, teeter-totters, a jungle gym, and a roller coaster. But their favorite is a family project—a six-foot-high marble chase with several tracks, in which the falling marbles spin wheels, race around loops, and set off chain reactions.

Myles is a Legomaniac, who uses his growing collection to create elaborate scenes with pirate ships, castles, island forts, and an occasional plane or spaceship. He likes to start by following directions, then to take the models apart and construct his own versions. To keep Myles's scenes from taking over the house, his parents built him a large, low table, supported by crates in which he keeps his supplies.

Katie is not much interested in building toys, but she loves to build with sand. Most of the time she makes castles or cakes, but occasionally she gets more creative. She and Kate were particularly proud of their "upside-down volcano," a cone-shaped hole in the sand.

Tessa loved to build with blocks in first and second grade and often led the group in creating garages, hospitals, theme parks, and fanciful castles. Her third-and-fourth-grade classroom lacked blocks, but when one of the boys brought in his Beanie Baby kangaroo to show his friends, Tessa decided it needed a house. Books, pillows, sheets of paper, and a couple of borrowed hats were pressed into service, and soon the baby kangaroo had a cradle, a desk, and a roof over his head.

COOKING

Many five-to-eight-year-olds love to cook, and some become quite competent. Both mothers and fathers enjoy cooking with their children. When we asked parents for examples of fun things that they did with their children that they thought other parents would enjoy, many mentioned cooking together.

As with Legos and other construction toys, some children like to follow the directions, while others prefer to make their own creations. Children who like to follow recipes often become fascinated with the techniques of cooking; they learn to grease pans, measure carefully, crack and even separate eggs

without breaking the yolks, flip pancakes, knead bread, mix smooth batter, whip cream, and make perfect al dente pasta. Brenan, whose parents tended to cook simply, got interested in watching cooking shows on TV. He would then want to make the most elaborate recipes he could find. Caroline, always the first one awake in her family, learned to make her own breakfast of chocolate chip pancakes. She needed help with the stove for a while, but was so persistent in her practicing that eventually her parents conceded that she could safely make breakfast on her own.

For some children, the fun of inventing something new makes recipes irrelevant and may even outweigh what most adults would consider good taste. Greg invented "rainbow sandwiches," which he insisted on having for lunch each day. They consisted of mayonnaise, bologna, peanut butter, grape jelly, banana, and cream cheese, neatly arranged in layers. Rick included chocolate chips, bananas, and cheese in his "everything omelets."

Another fun cooking activity is decorating. Katie likes to help her grandmother arrange platters for lunch, making flowers and other designs with rolled-up cheese and cold cuts, grapes, pea pods, and baby carrots. Arran's favorite lunch is a mound of cottage cheese topped with honey, on which he makes a face with raisins, carrot slices, bits of fruit, and Cheerios. David likes to spoon his yogurt into an ice cream cone and decorate it with sprinkles and banana slices. Kori liked to draw faces on her hamburgers with ketchup and mustard and to help her mother make designs with the spaghetti sauce on the top layer of lasagna. And of course, decorating cakes, brownies, or gingerbread houses with candies, dried fruits, and small toys is a special birthday or holiday treat.

STORYTELLING, JOKES, AND SPOOFS

"Would you like to hide in my tent tonight and I'll tell you a real scary ghost story?" asked Kevin's friend, Karl. "I'd like to," Kevin explained, "but I'm about to catch a cold."

For most children between five and eight, storytelling is a way of pretending. It allows children to replay a significant happening or invent a new scenario where they can be the hero.

Caroline, age eight, closeted herself in her room and wrote the following delightful fairy tale. Although her writing is sophisticated for an eight-year-old, it is a good example of how young children write themselves into a story as the central character.

MY LITTLE DOLL, SUE, *by Caroline Segal*

I sat there in my tiny chair. I was looking over my bed and saw a little doll. I ran over and picked her up. I ran out the door (almost running over the cat) into the kitchen to show Mom.

"That doll was your grandmother's when she was a little girl. She loved that doll," said Mom.

"I'm going to name her Sue and I'm going to take her out to play!" I said.

Della, my little sister, ran over to see Sue. "That's a gorgeous doll," she said to me.

"Her name is Sue," I said.

"Let's have a tea party for Sue!" said little Della.

"Sure," I finally said.

Della ran inside to get her doll, Lucy, and the tea party supplies. After the tea party, I lay Sue down on my bed and put a blanket over her made from a towel. I sat down next to her examining her small head. As I examined, I imagined. As I imagined, I admired. I saw her grow into a life-sized person and a friend. She opened her eyes. She stood up and looked confused.

"Hi! I'm Sue. What is your name?" Sue asked me in a quiet but beautiful voice.

"My name is Caroline, and just a few minutes ago you were my doll! You had a tea party with my sister, Della, her doll named Lucy and me," I said to Sue, as she stepped closer.

"I don't believe this!" she said. "I just had a tea party with my sister, Lucy, Lucy's doll Della, and my doll Caroline!"

Sue and I hooked arms and skipped down the buttermilk path. We skipped on and on until we reached a fence. There was a hole in the fence. We ran through the hole in the fence. I ran in after Sue. We ran down a set of stairs. We jumped over a snake and ducked under a low tree branch. Finally, I was out of breath. I decided to go over to a tree and pick a few chocolate chip cookies. "I didn't have lunch yet," I said in a rushed voice.

Sue spread the blanket I gave her on the floor. We set the cookies down and ate them like pigs. Next we found ourselves in a dark and scary cave. Sue pulled me behind a rock. I suddenly heard a growl. A bear walked right in front of me. I ducked down as low as possible, and I suddenly felt Sue getting smaller and smaller by the second.

The next thing I knew, I was ducking behind my little chair holding Sue down on the ground. I got up, dressed Sue and took her to the kitchen for lunch.

"How was your day?" Mom asked me.

"The best day of my life!" I said to my mother, smiling at my little doll, Sue.

I'll never forget that day. I sometimes try to do it all over again, but it never works the same.

Like Caroline, Kevin had a knack for telling stories. In contrast to Caroline, he did not make himself a central character. His stories were like jokes with a punch line, and his intention was to make people laugh.

There was a fly who wanted to be an astronaut. He went into a rocket ship with astronauts. The astronauts went to sleep. The fly woke up. He saw the moon. He got out of the rocket ship and jumped on the moon. He put up a flag. He said, "this is a small step for a fly but a giant step for fly-kind."

While seven- and eight-year-olds are likely to create their own original stories, younger children are more apt to retell a familiar story or invent a different version of a story told by a parent. At bedtime, Kate's father always told her a story with a moral about an animal who got into difficulty and had to find a way out. Kate would extend the bedtime routine by telling her father a story. Her story was usually a version of her father's, with different animals, but a similar moral. Jessica's father told stories in which children are carried away to a magical place by a balloon. When Jessica took her turn telling the story, the magical place where the children landed became more and more preposterous.

Many of the stories that five- and six-year-olds tell are a kind of running dialogue that accompanies their pretend play. Katie loves to play with her grandmother's chess set. She bounces the queen and king across the board. "Want to ride? I'll get the horses," the king says to the queen. "Get on your horse. It's time to go back to our castle."

In addition to telling stories, most five-to-eight-year-olds appreciate and repeat simple jokes. Knock-knock jokes may make grown-ups groan, but children from five to eight love them. In order to appreciate the humor in a knock-knock joke, children must be skilled enough with language to recognize a pun. Sarah, age five, told the same knock-knock joke over and over and always expected a laugh. "Knock-knock." "Who's there?" "Banana." "Banana who?" "Banana." "Banana who?" "Orange." "Orange who?" "Orange you glad I didn't say banana again?"

The "Why did the chicken cross the street?" jokes are somewhat more sophisticated than the knock-knock jokes and are preferred by seven- and eight-year-olds. The humor of the chicken jokes derives from the unexpected punch line. "Why did the chicken cross the street?" "To get the Chinese newspaper." "You get it?" "No." "Neither do I. I get *USA Today*."

While children enjoy repeating someone else's jokes, they would usually rather make up their own. Almost every parent we spoke to talked about their children making nonsensical jokes and expecting everyone to laugh. Benjamin and his sister have developed a joke-telling routine. Benjamin invents a nonsense joke like, "The hot-dog needs a hamburger head!" His sister taps the drumroll and they both laugh hysterically.

Sonia figured out how to create a play on words but couldn't quite pull off a punch line. "What would you do if the teacher told you to take the gum out of your mouth when a train went by and said, 'Choo-choo'?"

Endre's pun came out backwards. "Why didn't the elephant wear his trunk to the beach?" "Because he wanted to go in the water."

Brenan, having created several jokes that no one could get, spontaneously created one that worked. "Mom, see that broken traffic light up there?" "Someone went through it."

Ethan specialized in riddles. Instead of asking his mother for a fork at dinner one night, he asked her for a "quad stabber." When his mother asked him if he wanted orange juice or milk for dinner, Ethan replied, "If the first thing is potato and the second is apple, I want potato."

The sense of humor of a five-to-eight-year-old is reflected not only in jokes and riddles but also in their spoofs.

Becky changes her voice when she answers the telephone and pretends she is someone else. Mark, who lives in Florida, told his mother that he was putting on his jacket so that he could go out in the snow. When Bobby's father told him it was bedtime, Bobby grinned. "I can't go to bed, I'm on my way out to drive the car." Leigh wrote a letter to her mother's friend and signed it, "Your secret admirer." Then on the back of the letter she wrote, "Ha Ha, I'm Leigh!"

ANSWERS TO PARENTS' QUESTIONS

How can I promote my child's creativity?

Creative children are fun to live with. They look at the world with fresh eyes, identify incongruities, investigate and experiment, make new discoveries, perform, and produce. Children express their creativity in many different ways. They may be budding musicians, artists, builders, inventors, storytellers, or playwrights. Parents of creative children are likely to be creative themselves, to have a good sense of humor, to introduce their children to a wide variety of experiences, to tolerate messiness, and to stock their homes with basic materials that invite creative activities—store-bought materials like crayons, markers, paints, scissors, paste, construction paper, craft paper, Play-Doh, brads, pipe cleaners, string, and soda straws, and recycled materials like different-sized boxes, gift wrap, paper towel spindles, egg cartons, fabric scraps, wood scraps, bubble wrap, buttons, old socks, shoe laces, old magazines, and catalogues.

My child loves to draw, and is a very good artist. Should I give her lessons, or will that kill her creativity?

Although it is not necessary to give children art lessons at a young age in order to develop their talent, some children enjoy participating in a drawing class. Here are some cautions:

- Make sure that your child has a real interest in joining an art class.
- Do not enroll your child in an art class if she is already overscheduled.
- Select an instructor who encourages creativity and does not make corrections by drawing on the children's pictures.
- If you find that the drawings of all the children look the same, withdraw your child from the class.

My child is losing interest in drawing because he doesn't think he's good enough. Is there anything I can do to keep this skill alive?

It is not uncommon for children with artistic talent to become overconcerned with realism and accuracy. Their focus on being correct makes them critical if their drawings don't meet their self-imposed standards. Encourage your child to be playful with his drawings. He can draw to music, draw cartoon figures, draw distorted versions of familiar objects like cars, trucks, animals, houses, and trees, or play a game like Pictionary, where a child has to draw objects in 20 seconds and see if his friends can identify what he has drawn. Other ways to maintain an interest in drawing include encouraging your child to draw designs or taking him to an art museum and letting him sketch a well-known painting.

PLAY IDEAS

- Play a range of music for your child, including classical, jazz, folk, and popular music.
- Let your child make a tape of favorite songs to listen to in the car or for a family sing-along.
- Tape a large piece of paper to a wall and create a group or family multimedia mural. Contributions can be drawn or pasted onto the mural.
- Read Dr. Seuss's books *If I Ran the Zoo* and *On Beyond Zebra*. Make your own menagerie with miniature marshmallows and toothpicks, pipe cleaners, clay, or recycled materials.
- Make a sturdy portable base for building with Legos or other kinds of blocks.
- Play instrumental music to help set the mood while your child is cooking, painting, or building.
- Frame some of your child's artworks and display them in a special place. Or let your child be in charge of choosing a picture to put up in the place of honor, and changing it

when he makes one he likes better. Keep unframed but special pictures in a file or portfolio.

- Create a group drawing on a large sheet of paper. You can collaborate on deciding what to draw, or play a game in which no talking is allowed and people take turns adding to the picture without knowing what it is meant to be.
- Recycle preschool inset puzzles by tracing around animal or object pieces and drawing an appropriate background. Or draw the background first and then glue on the pieces.
- Collect shells, pebbles, seed pods, small leaves, pieces of bark, flat stones, and other interesting objects on a nature walk or outing. Use your collection to decorate puppets, drawings, murals, and "treasure boxes." Or make a simple picture frame for a photo or drawing of an outing, using cardboard or tongue depressors. Decorate the frame by gluing on some of the objects you found.
- Create an interesting mosaic by drawing a simple picture and "coloring" it by gluing on different kinds of beans and pasta.
- Play some storytelling games:
  - *Fortunately/Unfortunately:* Begin a story such as the following: "One day, a boy was walking along the street. Fortunately, it was a nice sunny day. Unfortunately . . ." The next player adds an unfortunate occurrence, and then says, "Fortunately . . ." The next player continues with a fortunate event, which is reversed on the next turn with an unfortunate one. Continue until the story comes to a natural end.
  - *Story-Go-Round:* Start a story and stop at an exciting point. Let your child continue the story until he runs out of ideas. Then you or another child can take up the story again. You might begin with something like, "Once there was a little girl who went for a walk with her mother. All of a sudden, they came to a meadow. The girl saw a beautiful

flower and ran to pick it. 'Wait,' said her mother, 'it might be magic!' But it was too late. The girl picked the flower and . . ."

• *Story Bag:* Put some unusual objects in a bag, for example: a button, a rubber animal, a clothing tag, an eraser, a ring, a piece of chalk, a magnet. Then let your child choose three things and tell a story that includes them. Your child will enjoy making story bags for you. If your child is reading, you can put some words instead of objects in the bag.

• Help your child make totem poles, story necklaces, or mobiles by drawing characters or key props from a familiar story, cutting them out, and gluing them onto paper towel spindles or attaching them to a piece of string in order of their appearance in the story. You and your child can retell the story, using the totem pole, necklace, or mobile for cues.

• Help your child make puppets using old socks or paper plates and sticks. Use the puppets to retell a familiar story.

• Help your child make a book of your family's favorite jokes. You can "publish" it by making copies and giving them as holiday presents to extended family members.

• If your child likes to cook, encourage him to invent some simple dishes. Pasta dishes, omelets, sandwiches, salads, vegetable soups, and fruit pies are usually safe bets that can be varied and still taste good. Create a cookbook with your child's recipes.

• Spread peanut butter on rice cakes and let your child decorate them with raisins, bits of cereal, and small pieces of fruit or vegetable.

• Shop together for a theme lunch or dinner that you and your child can make as a special family treat. You might include something from every continent, traditional foods from a particular country, a rainbow meal or a meal that is all one color, one favorite dish for each person in the family, or a food you have never tried. Your child may want to make a menu or table decoration to go with the special meal.

- Buy a children's cookbook or party book, or borrow one from the library.
- Watch cooking shows or videotapes with your child.
- Make edible clay with your child, using one of the following recipes:

PRETZEL DOUGH

Materials:

1 pkg. yeast	large bowl
1½ cups warm water	spoon
1 teaspoon salt	cookie sheet
1 tablespoon sugar	brush
4 cups flour	
1 egg beaten	

Process:

1. Preheat oven to 350°
2. Measure warm water into large bowl.
3. Sprinkle on yeast and stir until soft.
4. Add salt, sugar, flour.
5. Mix and knead dough with hands.
6. Roll and twist into any desired shapes.
7. Place on greased cookie sheet.
8. Brush with beaten egg.
9. Sprinkle with salt (optional).
10. Bake 12 to 15 minutes at 350°.

PEANUT BUTTER PLAYDOUGH

Materials: 1 cup peanut butter
½ cup dry nonfat milk
½ cup honey

Process: Mix all parts together with your hands until stiff.

CINNAMON DOUGH

Materials: 2 cups flour   bowl
1 cup salt   cookie sheets
5 teaspoons cinnamon   bread board
¾ to 1 cup warm water   plastic wrap

Process:

1. Mix flour, salt, and cinnamon in bowl.
2. Make a well in center.
3. Pour in water.
4. Mix with hands until dough forms a ball.
5. Knead on lightly floured board until smooth and satiny, about 5 minutes.
6. Wrap in plastic and refrigerate 20 minutes before using.
7. Use as you would any clay.
8. Excellent for cookie-cutter ornaments, rolled ¾-inch thick and baked at 350° for 1 hour, until hard.

Variations:

• Press dough through garlic press to make hair.
• Make a hole in the ornament before baking. Thread ribbon through to hang.

• Make homemade clay that your child can use to craft permanent sculptures. Try one of the following recipes:

SOAPSUDS CLAY

Materials:
¾ cup soap powder such as Ivory Snow
1 tablespoon warm water
electric mixer or hand mixer

Process:

1. Mix soap and water in bowl.
2. Beat with mixer until claylike.
3. Mold clay into objects.
4. Dries to hard finish.

Variation:

1. Beat 2 parts soap powder to 1 part water.
2. Spread like frosting on heavy cardboard.
3. Dries to a rubbery, smooth surface overnight.

SHAMPOO DOUGH

Materials:
¾ cup flour   bowl
¼ cup glue   paint (optional)
¼ cup thick shampoo

Process:

1. Mix all ingredients in bowl.
2. Knead.
3. Add more flour if needed.
4. Model, or roll out and cut.
5. Dry.
6. Paint if desired.

CHAPTER 6

Pretend Play

~~~~~~

Scooper Dooper is my friend.
He always wants to play.
And when I try to banish him,
He will not go away.

We sometimes go outside at night
And try to name the stars.
And then we board a rocket ship
And travel up to Mars.

We sometimes go exploring
In a strange and dangerous land.
I'm not afraid of anything,
When Scooper's in my hand.

My mother keeps on telling me
That Scooper's just pretend.
But even if my mom is right
He's still my favorite friend.

Pretend play is usually associated with the preschool years, but, like the old fisherman, it fades a little but never dies. Whether they are telling a ghost story, arranging a collection of baseball cards, or staging a dance recital in a backyard tent, children five to eight are creating and elaborating their imaginary world. Interestingly enough, when asked about their children's pretending, parents often tell us that they think their

children pretend but that they do it silently or behind closed doors. We cannot infer, however, that children are embarrassed about their pretending. For most, but not all children, pretending is a special way to have fun with a friend. Parents may be called on to serve as an appreciative audience when children put on a performance, but they are seldom invited to assume a role. Many children also derive special enjoyment from solitary pretending, where they can make the rules and control the flow of ideas without having to take anyone else's wishes into account.

Pretend play in the five-to-eight-year age range takes on different forms. Children may assume the role of play director: setting the scene, talking for miniature characters as they move them up and down, or describing to an imaginary audience what the characters are doing. An even more popular pretend play mode is acting out a role. Children may be astronauts, dancers, caregivers, zoo keepers, Pocahontas or Robin Hood, parents or teenagers, teachers, chefs, or veterinarians. They may bring in armloads of props to support their pretend play, animate the first object they find, or create an imaginary companion.

We begin this chapter by looking at the two major types of pretending, actor play and dressing-up, where the child assumes a role, and director play, where the child speaks for or to the characters, moves them around, and directs the show. We then look at types of imaginative play that are less common but still typical of five-to-eight-year-olds, invisible friends, the re-emergence of pretending in children who had dropped it for other pursuits, and enduring worlds created jointly by close friends or relatives.

ACTOR PLAY AND DRESSING UP

"Man overboard!" Darryl shouted, as he threw his stuffed animal out of the tree branch canoe. "Quick man, throw out the rope! There are alligators in this water!"

"Oh, my God!" his friend Vincent screamed. "He's already been attacked!"

"Call the Coast Guard! He's hurt real bad; there's blood coming out of him."

"Too late, the alligator killed him dead."

"No," Darryl insisted, "he's not really dead. He's just pretending to be dead!"

Actor-type pretending is particularly popular with five-to-eight-year-old children. Although girls and boys sometimes share a pretend theme, the pretend themes of girls are undeniably different from the play themes of boys. Boys like Darryl and Vincent like fast action themes, with danger lurking everywhere. Other boys play good guy/bad guy with a gang of friends, play football against an imaginary team, or assume the identity of a dangerous character. Girls prefer to dress up a Barbie doll, put on a dance recital, or act out a fairy tale or a familiar scene. "Would you like to hear about our specials for the night?" waitress Brittany asks, as she pours her customer an imaginary glass of wine. "You be the troll," Lisa says to her mother. "Joey and I will be the two Billy Goats Gruff."

Caroline and Katie were playing with Tinkertoys. Just like many boys, they began the play by making guns, running through the house, and making "pow-pow" noises. When they reached the kitchen where their grandmother was sitting, Caroline told her what they were doing. "We made magic guns. We're going to shoot the bad guys. When we shoot our guns sleeping dust comes out. The sleeping dust gets on the bad guys and makes them fall asleep. When they wake up they are good guys and they help us shoot the bad guys. We have a hundred pockets full of sleeping dust and every time a bad guy turns good we give him sleeping dust so he can help us and we bought a hundred more bags of sleeping dust and now we have enough."

"I found the oldest and the baddest bad man," Katie added, "and I shot him with my sleeping dust." Even though Caroline and Katie were acting out a gun-play theme, the play took on a decidedly feminine twist.

School play, popular with both boys and girls in the preschool years, is likely to continue in the elementary years with girls but not with boys. Katie, at six, discovered a unique way of playing school. Her mother's bathroom has a three-way mirror, and when you pull the bathroom door to the right angle you can see six reflections of yourself. Katie spent hours standing in front of the mirror teaching school to each of the six Katies. One Katie always knew the right answer, but the "Katie Kid" Katie could never remember that two times five is ten.

Caroline, like Katie, loves to play school. She sets up her dolls on the floor opposite a chalkboard that lists the day's assignments. Next she distributes paper to each of her pupils, instructs them to write a story, and then collects and corrects

their papers. "No boys are in my class," she tells her mother. "All they do is cause problems."

Jessica and her sister, Susan, told us that they love to act out stories. Jessica plays Snow White because she has dark hair, and Susan, who is blonde, plays Cinderella. Inevitably, their playtime is spent trying on different costumes that they keep in a suitcase. By the time they have decided on the most appropriate costume, their mother reports, they are usually ready to move on to another activity.

Peter and his brother Danny also like to act out stories, but they get their scripts from television shows and movies more often than from books. Whenever their parents take them to a new movie, Peter and Danny repeat lines they remember, using appropriate voices, all the way home. They then choose roles and act out their favorite scenes.

Peter also engages in his own form of dress-up play. An avid sports fan, he loves to watch games on television while dressed in appropriate regalia. During football season, Peter borrows his mother's shoulderpads and stuffs them under his Green Bay Packers jersey, dons his street hockey helmet, and cradles his football as he kneels down to watch a game. His hockey-watching outfit is even more elaborate: a Rangers T-shirt covered by a ski parka, his Roller Blading knee and elbow pads, the street hockey helmet, and a baseball glove. Dressed as the goalie, Peter imitates the "great saves" that he sees on TV.

Camping out is a favorite theme for both boys and girls. The necessary paraphernalia may be a blanket, a pillow, a flashlight, a comic book, a large bag full of snacks, and a real or pretend tent. Ned and his friends love to pretend that they are camping in the woods. They build a fort out of porch furniture and pretend it is a tent. Then they make plans for foraging in the deep dark forest, surviving on wild berries and tree sap, and protecting themselves from the wild animals that are likely to attack them.

Another theme, shared by boys and girls, is impersonating a media star. Jenna dresses herself up in a fancy outfit, stands in front of the mirrors, sings in a low voice, and pretends she's Whitney Houston. Alice puts on sunglasses, strums her play

guitar, sings in a scratchy voice, and introduces herself as the famous Bob Dylan. Danny, an inveterate clown, likes to sing while he plays. As soon as an audience appears, he raises his voice two octaves in a parody of whichever female rock star has popularized the song he is singing.

A favorite actor-type play, particularly for five- and six-year-olds, is pretending to be an animal. Benjamin spent a whole day oinking like a pig, having assigned the role of the big bad wolf to his mother. "You got to huff and puff," he told his mother, "but you can't blow my house down because it's made out of bricks."

Lisa dresses up in black tights and a black shirt and barks as she walks on all fours around the house. Her friend Jason is her master. "Sit," he orders her, but dog Lisa will not obey. Katie and Caroline pretend to be cats, licking their "paws," meowing, rolling over on their backs, lapping up "milk," and rubbing up against every adult in sight.

DIRECTOR PLAY

In director play, the children arrange and animate a miniature world. Some children talk for the miniature characters; some animate them silently. Others take on the role of narrator, moving the characters around the scene and describing what is taking place. Still other children, like true directors, talk to the characters and tell them what to do.

Alan and his brother Jeff spend every summer going to one or two national parks, and have amassed an impressive collection of rubber animal souvenirs. One of their favorite activities is playing zoo, which involves moving the animals in and out of block cages. "Okay, Eagle, you can fly out of the cage but don't leave the park." "Puffin, it's time for dinner. Do you want to eat with the walrus and the Orca whale? Okay, but don't gobble your food."

Talking for the Characters

Talking for miniature characters in director-type play is more typical of five-year-olds than older children. Alice, age five, had a collection of playscapes permanently set up in her bedroom. One was a farm, complete with a barn, a feeding trough, fences, a farmer, and an impressive set of farm animals. Alice sat down on the floor, took the animals out of the barn, and grouped the chickens, cows, pigs, and sheep. She began her pretend story by picking up the farmer. Alice squeaked as she made the farmer jump up and down. "Okay, cows, milking time, go into the barn." Next she picked up a cow in her other hand. "Moo, moo. I don't want to go in the barn. I want to eat my hay. Moo, moo." "Okay, eat your supper. After supper you get milking." "Come here, hen. You lay two eggs for my breakfast." "Cluck, cluck. I don't want to. I'm going to fly away." Alice continued the play for a good half hour until all the animals did the farmer's bidding.

Animating Silently

A variant on talking for the characters is to animate them silently. Several parents told us that their children played this way. Endre, for example, likes to set up scenes with his Power Rangers and engage them in imaginary fights. Brenan liked to bash his Muscle Men characters together, making them fight. Occasional squeaks, but no words, would escape his lips as he played. Steven likes to build elaborate boats and barges with Legos or scraps of wood, which he pilots silently through apparently dangerous waters.

Brittany's parents gave us detailed descriptions of her actor play and of her backyard experiments with strange concoctions like mud bread and acorn soup. But they were at a loss to explain what she does with her dolls. "She goes into her

room by herself, and just plays silently. I often find the dolls on the floor, or on her pillow, with all kinds of small objects that I guess she uses for their toys. When something is missing in the house, the first place I look is Brittany's room. Most of the time, I find it in a doll's hand, or in a little basket with other odds and ends."

Narrating the Story

Justin, age six, plays silently when he's by himself, but only when he can't snare an audience. He corners his mother's friend one day and begins an elaborate story, using his miniature characters to illustrate. Justin picks up a toy dinosaur skeleton, demonstrates its movable parts, and begins his narrative. "This dinosaur is really fierce. He eats meat, but no one can eat him cause he doesn't have any meat, only bones. See, he can make himself look dead, but he's not. When he eats he takes the good stuff and it goes in his bones, and the poop comes out in a ball. Give me that stuffed dog. Ooh. The dinosaur ate the dog. Here comes the keeper to clean up. Ooh, he ate the keeper. He needs to be in a cage so he can't get out."

Justin's story continued for a full half hour, with some parts repeated to accommodate improvements that he made as he went along, until his mother decided that her friend had had enough. At that point, Justin taped the dinosaur and some army guys onto a cardboard "raft." After explaining his invention to his family, he quietly sailed it out the front door, and continued directing his story on the front porch.

Talking to the Characters

A third way to enact director-style play is to talk to the characters. This play style is used most frequently when children are playing with dolls or stuffed animals. "Oh, Barbie," says Jenna, "you look beautiful. Is Ken taking you to the dance tonight? You had a fight with Ken? I can't believe it. He doesn't like your blue dress? No problem, let's put on your pink dress and your silver high heel shoes. Okay?"

"Hurry, Cyclops," calls Endre. "Wolverine's in trouble. Magneto's beating him bad. You've got to get there quick."

FOUND TOYS AND IMAGINARY PLAYMATES

While director and actor play are most popular with five-to-eight-year-olds, there are children who continue to enjoy animating nonrepresentational objects or playing with an imaginary friend.

Xavier and his sister were going on a long car drive. Their mother had not allowed them to bring toys along because she wanted them to watch the scenery and listen to classical music.

Her plan did not work out. Xavier and his sister took off their shoelaces. At first they pretended the shoelaces were snakes, wriggling them around the back seat and staging a couple of snake fights. Next, they took off their shoes, put their shoelaces inside them, and pretended they were eating boiling hot dishes of spaghetti.

While imaginary friends are likely to appear at three years old and disappear at four, some children five and over continue to enjoy playing with invisible friends. These children are perfectly aware that their friends are make-believe, but they want their parents and siblings to behave as if they are real. A father who sits on an imaginary friend is likely to get reprimanded. "Daddy, why did you sit on that chair? You are crushing poor Boolabutt!"

Sonia's invisible and stuffed animal friends are part of the family. Elmo, a well-loved Muppet toy, joins the family for breakfast each morning. Sonia's mother Nancy talks for Elmo when Sonia or her other mother Sharon asks him what he'd like to eat. "Invisible" (but, according to Sonia, definitely not imaginary) friends often come along on family outings. Esther is from India, like a child in Sonia's class, and always wants to be first to try something new. Kerry and Jimmy are longtime companions who accompany Sonia everywhere. Kerry, like Sonia's big sister, is a super athlete, while Jimmy is somewhat timid and takes longer to master physical challenges. Although Sonia has created a fine collection of imaginary friends, she continues to search for new ones. She loves to go to the cemetery and read the names on the tombstones. The names she reads off become her "invisible people," and she includes them in fantasy play along with her "invisible friends."

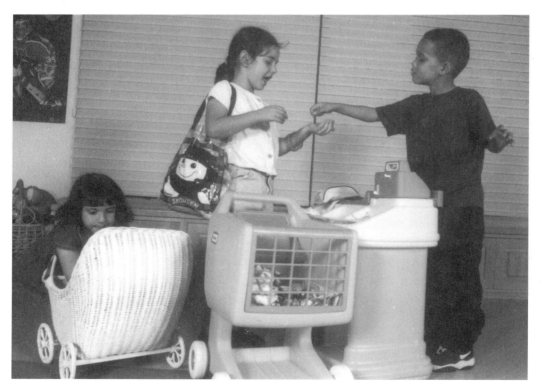

REEMERGENCE OF PRETENDING

Many seven- and eight-year-olds become convinced that they are too big for pretending, especially when the pretending involves nurturing a doll or stuffed animal. Worried that other kids will laugh at them, they may put away their "baby" toys in favor of sports, video games, and scary mystery stories. Yet, with a little encouragement or permission, the pretending may reemerge.

During his preschool years, Xavier showed little interest in pretending, and very little interest in toys. His favorite activity was talking with his parents. He loved to ask sophisticated questions, and listened attentively to their answers. As an unusually intellectual child, Xavier felt that pretending and toy play were babyish, and he had little time for them.

Much to his parents' surprise, Xavier's pretending reemerged at six years old. Rather than looking at this as regression, his parents recognized that Xavier had found ways to pretend that fit in with his intellectual proclivities. Xavier dressed up as a magician as a way of adding to the authenticity of his magic tricks. He developed a hieroglyphic code that allowed him to converse with his friends in a secret language that no one but he and his friends could understand. Most surprisingly, Xavier, influenced perhaps by his baby sister, developed a strong attachment to a stuffed teddy bear.

"I have decided to name my teddy bear 'Apretable,'" Xavier announced one day, because "Apretable" is Spanish for "squeezable." "Would you like to play Clue with me and Apretable?" Xavier asked his father a few days later. "You know he's very smart." Xavier sat his teddy bear on the chair beside him as he and his father sat down to play Clue. "Who do you suppose is going to be the guilty character?" his father asked, as they started the game. Xavier answered immediately. "Apretable

and I think it is going to be the redhead." As long as pretending was part of an intellectual game, from Xavier's point of view, it was all right to pretend.

When Xavier's friend Kyle came over to play, rather than immediately taking him to the Nintendo game, Xavier invited Kyle to play with his new remote-control car. Although Xavier had never played with cars and trucks when he was younger, the remote-control car appealed to him. After all, the remote-control car was an engineering marvel, which fit very well with his image of himself as a great inventor.

Ned's parents told us a similar story. "Ned has started playing with his army guys again," Ned's mother tells us, "since his new baby-sitter, Jody, is willing to do it with him. He got down an old bat cave that he hasn't used since in preschool, and now he sets up all kinds of battles. Last year he only wanted to play sports, so this aspect of his development got put on hold. I think it's something he needs to complete."

"I'm bringing my tiger to school today, cause we're studying India," eight-year-old Chad explains to the carpool driver, just in case someone might think he still plays with stuffed animals. "Hi, Tiger," the carpool mom responds. "I hope you like it at school. Can you do any tricks?" Soon Chad's tiger is showing off cartwheels, triple flips, and tail walking, and Chad is tenderly making sure that he doesn't get hurt.

A teacher's permission can be even more powerful. Arran's combined third-and-fourth-grade class had been reading chapter books with personified animal characters when one of the boys brought in his stuffed kangaroo. A lot of the children had admired this "cute" character, and some had even helped to build it a house. Seizing the opportunity, the teacher assigned creative writing for homework that night. "Choose an animal character and write a description of it. Tomorrow we're going to work in groups. Each group will write a story that uses all their animal characters. If you have a stuffed animal like the one you describe, you can bring it to school if you want." Two weeks later, the classroom was still inhabited by stuffed animals. Stories of their exploits were posted on the walls, but these paled beside the stories that were being played out before and after school, during breaks, and on the playground.

ENDURING WORLDS

Whether they prefer actor-type or director-type play, siblings, cousins, and close friends who visit regularly may create play worlds that endure for a long time. Brittany and her best friend dressed up as princesses every time they got together. For two years their game and costumes became more elaborate, until they fell into a routine of rehearsing and then putting on a show at each visit, complete with tickets and a program, with their mothers as the audience.

Jennifer and Kori, cousins who visited several times a year, developed a ritual of creating elaborate worlds with train sets, blocks, and miniature figures at their Nana's house. One day they built a summer camp, Camp Jennikoriana, which they imagined they would run together for their younger siblings and cousins. This camp was rebuilt, rearranged, and elaborated on subsequent visits. Their shared fantasy grew more intricate over the next several years, as they decided to open the camp to handicapped children and jointly planned its activity schedule.

Arran and Myles, friends who played together after school several days each week, enjoyed building Lego worlds, such as castles, pirate worlds, and occasionally space worlds. They developed their own system for separating "bad guys" and "good guys" who would fight each other, get injured and need hospital treatment, and sometimes recover to fight another day.

Kori and Brenan, three years apart, developed a shared fantasy of the "invisible people." Together, they fought these evil aliens with the elaborate Lego spaceships that Kori designed or that Brenan made following the directions. Outdoors, Kori and Brenan pretended that their jungle gym was a ship, and that the Invisible People were attacking them. They played a similar game on the top of their bunk bed, enlisting the help of their stuffed animals in warding off evil aliens. This shared play was a compromise; Kori always got to be "captain," controlling the play and telling her little brother what to do. Brenan didn't mind this, as long as they played out his favorite themes—fighting, aliens, and outer space. Kori was willing to put up with the fighting as long as she got to play out rescue/hospital and exploration/adventure fantasies. And, of course, having the invisible people as enemies meant that neither Kori nor Brenan had to be the bad guy.

ANSWERS TO PARENTS' QUESTIONS

My child likes to hide away and play by herself. I'd love to know what she is imagining, but I don't want to interrupt. Is there a way I can have access to her imaginative world without invading her privacy?

If you probe a child about her pretend play, you are sending out the wrong messages. Many children are secretive about their pretending not because they feel that it is babyish but because they don't want grown-ups intervening in their fantasy life. However, you can find opportunities to share pretend play with your child without trespassing on her private world. Play a computer game that has a fantasy theme, read a classic children's book, such as *Winnie the Pooh, James and the Giant Peach*, or *Alice in Wonderland*, that combines fantasy with humor, or join her in a building project in which you create a fantasy scene together.

My child at six years old is fearful of many things. He is afraid of going places without me, he worries about storms, and he hasn't gotten over his fear of monsters lurking in the house. How can I alleviate his fears?

Some children are temperamentally more fearful than others. The best way to help your son manage his fears is to talk openly about them. If your child is fearful of separating from you, talk about ways that would help him feel safer. Would he like you to write down the telephone number of where you will be so he can always be in touch with you? Would he like you to telephone him every hour?

If your child is fearful about storms or other natural events, begin by discussing the fact that different weather conditions create problems in different parts of the country. If you live in a region where hurricanes are a potential problem, talk about all the ways that your family has of being safe during a hurricane.

If your child is afraid of monsters in his closet, let him know that monsters are just pretend but that sometimes children are afraid of things even though they know it is just pretend. An obvious way to handle the problem is keeping the light on in the closet. Another way is to buy your child a stuffed animal like a tiger or an alligator and tell him you have a new "just pretend" game for him to play. He can pretend that his new stuffed animal is real and that all the monsters are scared of it and will run out of the house. Fortunately, most children lose their fear of monsters by the time they are seven, when they can appreciate the difference between real and pretend.

My daughter loves Barbie dolls and keeps asking for Barbie things as presents. I don't want her to get the idea that real women look like Barbie or to buy into the materialistic, dating/entertainment culture that Barbie represents. What do you suggest?

Fortunately, the new renditions of Barbie convey a less materialistic teenager. There are Barbie dolls from different ethnic groups, enrolled in college, or engaging in activities and professions that don't promote the stereotypes of the dating/entertainment culture. In addition to buying a more varied collection of Barbie dolls, you can provide costumes and accessories that project a work-oriented image. Another idea suggested by a parent is to bring in other types of dolls as Barbie's friends.

My child seems stuck on war play, which makes me uncomfortable. Are there things I can do to help him develop other imaginative themes?

An interest in war play does not necessarily mean that your child is aggressive or will become aggressive. If you feel, however, that your child's war play has become stereotyped and noncreative, introduce new themes that are related to war play. Encourage your child to build a field hospital for wounded soldiers, go on a rescue mission for a lost companion, build shelters for families in a war zone, invent a new type of vehicle that keeps soldiers safe, or invent a concoction that makes the enemy fall asleep. Still another idea is to read myths, tall tales, or folktales in which the hero vanquishes or outwits the enemy. Your son may want to play out some of these tales with his war toys, or make appropriate costumes for himself or his action figures.

PLAY IDEAS

- Make a stage for children's performances. If you don't have a raised area or platform, you can use an old mattress or even a rug. For puppet shows, children can hide behind a couch or chair.
- Buy closeout fabrics—velvet strips, lace, satin—or thrift shop clothes and add them to your costume boxes.
- Introduce props for play themes from different times and cultures. These might include hats and costumes, percussion instruments, kitchen utensils, toys, dolls, postcards, and baskets. Read stories about children from that time or place, or folktales from the culture.
- Bubble guns and water pistols provide children with a way of engaging in harmless gunplay. "Guns" that children make themselves with Legos, Tinkertoys, or other snap-together materials lend themselves to creative uses. If your child shoots you with his "gun," you can introduce an unexpected element. "Oh, no! You just turned me green! And my nose is growing into a trunk! Quick, shoot me back to normal!"
- Encourage your child to "mix media." For example, you can create a chocolate factory together, using Legos, Tinker-

toys, and Erector Set pieces along with drinking straws, pipe cleaners, and aluminum foil.

• Encourage your child to use miniature characters not only to play out the stories they represent, but also for inventing alternate versions. Pooh Bear might want to plant a garden to grow honey; the Lion King's father could go on a fishing trip and come back; *Star Wars* characters could go on a rescue mission to a distant galaxy or save a planet from an approaching asteroid.

• Use a low set of shelves like a dollhouse. Set up rooms of the house, or scenes, such as a hospital, circus, school, playground, or work site.

• Collect old baby clothes, socks, scraps of material, yarn, and ribbon that children can use to make costumes for their dolls, stuffed animals, or action figures. Costumes don't have to be elaborate or sewn; children can usually tie or tape them on, or just cut armholes.

• Use boxes of varying sizes to make furniture for dolls or stuffed animals.

• Give your child's favorite dolls, stuffed animals, or action figures "presents" on special holidays or birthdays.

• Create a space where enduring play worlds can be left out. If space is in short supply, you can put a train set or Lego world on a large sheet of plywood with casters and roll it under a bed, keep bins or crates with building materials under a low table that can hold a permanent scene, arrange miniature characters on a windowsill, or turn the space under a bench or sideboard into a miniature garage or marketplace.

School Play

Caroline, age seven, is playing school with her dolls. She has written a class schedule on her white board: Morning Meeting, Reading, Math, Spelling, Recess, Lunch. "Come on, everybody," says Miss Caroline, "it's time to start the spelling bee. The first word is 'friendship.' Felicity?"

"F-R-E-N-D-S-H-I-P"

"No, I'm sorry. That's wrong. Molly?"

"F-R-E-I-N-S-H-I-P"

"You'll do better next time, Molly. Samantha?"

"F-R-I-E-N-S-H-I-P"

"You've almost got it. Addie?"

"F-R-I-E-N-D-S-H-I-P"

"Correct! Hooray for Addie."

Some children, like Caroline, love to play school. They

may mimic classroom routines, give themselves homework, "study about" a topic that interests them, initiate quiz games, even write out their own report cards.

But whether or not they play school, most five-to-eight-year-olds incorporate school-like activities—reading, writing, and arithmetic, as well as collecting facts and making science experiments and inventions—into their play.

READING

Learning to Read

When you're five, six, or seven, reading is a BIG deal. "I want to learn to READ!" shouts six-year-old Justin, when asked what things he wants to know about. Although he can read simple words and primers, he recognizes that he can't yet read real books on his own. He knows from watching his parents and older brothers that this ability will unlock a new world for him;

not only will he be able to find out the answers to all of his questions, but he, too, will be able to say with authority, "I'm right. See, it says so in this book."

Ethan, also six, has just mastered reading. Now he's full of new questions. "Mom, why did you write 'Empty' on that box?" "Why does the sign near the school say 'Go children slow'?" "Can we go to the library and get a book about stars and planets?" Ethan is so excited with his new skill that he tries to read everything—road signs, the comics that come in his Lego sets, even the tags on his new clothes. The books Ethan can read independently rarely contain enough information to satisfy his curiosity, as he is used to being read rather sophisticated passages by his parents in response to his requests for exotic information. Nevertheless, nothing beats the thrill of discovering information on his own.

Jessica, another six-year-old and a beginning reader, is more enamored with the sounds of words in books than with the information they contain. She's enjoying the process of learning to read, and likes simple books, like *Mac and Tab,* that she can read on her own. But her literary tastes are way beyond this level. Her mother often reads her classics: *Little Women, Anne of Green Gables, Mary Poppins, The Wizard of Oz.* Jessica enjoys the literary language, and will sometimes quote favorite lines or find ways to incorporate new vocabulary words into everyday conversation. Once, when Jessica's mother returned late from an evening meeting and asked, "Did you miss me?" Jessica responded with language worthy of a Victorian heroine: "I missed your gentle mommyish ways."

Jessica gets so wrapped up in the stories her parents read to her that she rarely wants them to stop. She identifies with the characters and takes their problems seriously. When a character in the book is treated unfairly, Jessica will become quite agitated and insist that they keep reading until the problem is resolved. She brags about her status as a "night owl"; often, her father falls asleep while reading to her and begins to say words that don't make sense. Jessica is always awake enough to catch the mistakes and to repeat them to her mother and sister in the morning.

Sonia, another six-year-old, has been reading since she was three. Her literary tastes are eclectic: she loves Dr. Seuss, Marc Brown's Arthur books, *Franklin the Turtle,* and *Harriet the Spy,* but she will read anything. She even checks out medical books from the school library. Although Sonia can read all of these books on her own, she still enjoys reading with her mother. Her favorite method is to take turns: Sonia reads a passage; her mother reads the rest of the page; or Sonia reads a page and her other mother reads the next three. Early reading has given Sonia a special status at school; she is often called upon to help other children, and very much enjoys this role.

Five-year-old Alice also has quite sophisticated literary tastes. She has just about outgrown the Curious George books, which used to be her favorites. Now she likes to listen to *The Little Prince* and to both children's and adult versions of the story of Prince Siddhartha, or Buddha. Alice likes to sit in her special chair and "read" books she knows, carefully retelling the story in detail as she turns the pages slowly. "I can't really read the words but I remember the story," she explains. She is so proud every time she finishes a book!

Six-year-old Christopher is a very competent reader. He loves books about kids his age, especially when they are playing sports or solving mysteries. But every time his parents suggest that he pick up a book, he resists. Once he gets started, however, they have a hard time getting him to put the book down!

For children who read late, reading in school can be trying. Adrian, a seventh grader, was asked to write an essay about a difficult or challenging experience. He told a painful story about being the only kid in his first-grade class who wasn't in a reading group. Neither his parents nor his teacher had been aware at the time of how hurt and left out Adrian was feeling.

Kori, who had a mild hearing loss, had difficulty learning to read phonetically. However she loved books and insisted that her parents read her favorites over and over. Memorizing the words helped Kori learn to read them herself, but for a long time she kept this skill a secret. She enjoyed being read to and was afraid her parents might stop when they found out she could do it on her own.

Brenan learned to read at two, while his best friend Nick struggled throughout first grade. By third grade, however, it was Nick who was recommending books to Brenan, a pattern that continued into their teenage years. As long as children continue to enjoy books, whether they learn to read at two or at seven and whether they achieve mastery through their own play or with the help of a tutor seems to make little difference in the long run.

Reading for Fun

Although many five-to-eight-year-olds resist the work of reading independently, almost all of them love being read to and like to participate in the reading by asking questions, predicting what will happen next, chiming in at familiar or predictable parts, following along, discussing details in the pictures, protesting when a sympathetic character is treated unfairly or asking for reassurance when a favorite character is in danger, even reading some words or passages or taking the part of one of the characters.

Most families set aside special times for reading or develop their own rituals. Conor's mother reads one story to Conor and any other kindergartners who want to listen before saying good-bye each morning. Todd's mother lies beside him for reading time each night. Fahran's father takes him to the library once a week to pick out books that they can read together. Kate, who is proud of her new reading skills, likes to read to her family each night before she gets ready for bed.

Ned's parents place the sports page by his cereal bowl every morning, knowing that Ned won't go to school until he has read about last night's soccer games. Jessica is especially thrilled when her parents vary the routine, reading good-night stories by flashlight in the backyard fort or serving breakfast—with a story—in the bathtub.

Peter likes to do his reading on the computer. He especially loves adventure games where he gets to choose what will happen next. Peter will plunge into a new game, even if he can't read all of the words, and often has it figured out while his parents are still reading the manual.

Children vary immensely in their literary tastes, but there are certain commonalities. Nearly all five-to-eight-year-olds enjoy humor. Five- and six-year-olds enjoy stories where the protagonists do silly things. They like the rhyme, rhythm, invented words, and cartoon illustrations in books by Dr. Seuss and in other beginner books. They enjoy absurdity, whether it comes in pictures with "mistakes," the actions of bumbling or clueless characters, ridiculously impossible happenings, or the playful language of a nonsense poem. They especially enjoy stories in which they can participate—by pointing out what is wacky or repeating an easily memorized rhyme or a tongue-twister like "Tikki-Tikki-Tembo—No Sa Rembo—Cherry Berry Ruchi—Pip Peri Pembo."

By age six, most children are able to appreciate simple puns. Joke and riddle books become popular, as do books like the Amelia Bedelia series, in which the humor turns on the misinterpretation of homonyms.

Seven- and eight-year-olds, while continuing to enjoy slap-stick, absurdity, and wordplay, also develop an appreciation for irony, parody, and caricature, and enjoy books that poke fun at foibles they see in themselves and those around them. Books like *Miss Nelson Is Missing* and *The True Story of the Big Bad Wolf,* which gain their humor through discrepancies between what a character says and what is really going on, become popular as children are able to understand when and why a character stretches the truth.

Fairy tales are also a favorite genre, especially for girls. The magical transformations, the triumph of good over evil, the vindication of children who outwit their parents, and the victories of small or weak characters over the powerful and corrupt have special appeal for children. Many children enjoy comparing different versions of familiar tales. These include classic or traditional renditions, Disney retellings, tales with similar plots from other cultures, and modern versions that twist the tales to make a feminist or anti-bias point or simply for humorous effect.

Myths have an appeal similar to that of fairy tales, and boys seem particularly drawn to their larger-than-life heroes. Tall tales become appealing when children develop the sophis-tication to appreciate exaggerated humor and regionally colorful language. Even more popular, because they are more accessible, are fantasy and science fiction series like *My Father's Dragon, The Indian in the Cupboard, The Chronicles of Narnia, The Tripods Trilogy,* and the *Moomintroll* books.

Although their parents do not consider them great literature, many children love to read books created from TV shows or movies, such as *Pocahontas, The Lion King,* or *Power Rangers.* These heavily illustrated books help children recall the story of the movie. Children enjoy rehearsing the entire plot or sharing favorite parts with family and friends. They may read the books over and over and also act out the story or replay it with miniature figures.

Mystery is another popular genre. Children especially enjoy seeing how child detectives like Nate the Great, Encyclopedia Brown, the Boxcar Children, Cam Jansen, and Junie Bee Jones outwit criminals and villains. They enjoy trying to guess the endings and like the fun facts that are often key to the solution. Some children devour the spooky variants of this genre, such as the Goosebumps books; others find them too scary or object to their rather trite writing style.

As much as children love stories, they also love facts. Historical fiction combines both, and many children love not only books like the American Girl series, which they can understand easily or even read on their own, but also books that stretch their vocabularies as well as their imaginations, such as *Little House on the Prairie, Little Women,* Virginia Hamilton's stories and folktales from slavery times. Biographies, too, allow children to learn history through a story. These often lead to new questions or to proud showing-off of knowledge as children discover facts that they are sure their parents don't know. "Mommy," asks Ned, after reading about Johnny Appleseed, "can you imagine what the world would be like if Johnny Appleseed hadn't lived?"

For some children, getting information is one of the main purposes of reading, and they will read, or at least leaf through, any book they can get their hands on in their area of special interest. Sports, dinosaurs, wild animals, space—whatever their passion, they will seek out books, magazines, newspaper articles, posters, computer programs, and videos that enable them to increase their store of specialized knowledge. Kevin likes to borrow his parents' medical books, especially the ones that show labeled skeletons or tell how babies are born. He has become an expert on anatomy and is teased and admired by his friends for his sophisticated anatomical vocabulary.

Other children are more eclectic in their information gathering. They may enjoy question-and-answer books, read the calendar or movie section of the newspaper religiously to see what is scheduled, check out library books about places they have visited or plan to visit, read children's cookbooks or craft books and follow the directions, browse through children's encyclopedias, or surf the web. They like books that combine humor with facts and new vocabulary words, such as *The Magic School Bus* series or *Frank and Ernest Play Baseball.*

Most children are also delighted by poetry, especially when it is clever or funny and has a light, lilting rhythm. Favorite authors include Eloise Greenfield, Mary Ann Hoberman, Shel Silverstein, David McCord, and Dr. Seuss. Some children like to memorize and recite poems, or read them in choral or call-and-response (turn-taking) fashion.

For many children, the best books of all are books about kids like them, or books in which animal characters behave like kids. Arthur and Curious George, Ramona the Pest and Harriet the Spy, Matt Christopher's child sports stars and Mercer Meyer's Little Monster—these characters face trials and tribulations that children can identify with, and often show them ways of resolving their own problems.

Many parents make a point of including multicultural books in their children's libraries, being sure that authors and protagonists represent a balanced mix of racial and ethnic groups, as well as both males and females. This balance has become easier to achieve in recent years, as a more diverse group of authors produce high-quality books and as prizes like the Coretta Scott King Award make it easy for parents to find the very best. For children of color, it is especially important that they read a variety of books in a variety of genres in which the authors and/or protagonists look or talk like they do. Endre, who loves the Goosebumps series, also seeks out African American books whenever he goes to the library or bookstore.

Like the movies and TV shows they watch, the books children read provide scripts and ideas for imaginative play. Six-year-old Sonia keeps a secret notebook—filled with stamps, stickers, pictures, and pretend writing—and imagines she is Harriet the Spy. Jessica and her younger sister Susan dress up as fairy-tale characters; brown-haired Jessica gets to be Snow White, while her blond sister is Cinderella. Callie and her best friend Maisha alternate between treating their American Girl dolls as modern kids for whom they make TVs as well as furniture and homework papers, and playing out historical scenarios based on the American Girl books. Kori looked to Judy Blume and Beverly Cleary, as well as Betty McDonald's Mrs. Piggle-Wiggle series for advice that would help her manage her dolls' conflicts as well as the real-life difficulties she faced in playing with peers or taking care of her younger brother and cousins.

WRITING

THE CAT NAMED CAROLINE
Once Their Was a Cat Named Caroline Who Can Do Every Thing And Can Talk. She Learned From A Lady Named Betty The End

This book, a present from five-year-old Caroline to her aunt, is a succinct summation of a weekend of play, in which Caroline, pretending to be a cat, begged for food in a mixture of English and meowing, performed circus tricks, curled up to be petted, played the piano, and won a skating contest.

Brittany's book captures a similar joy in playing with a friend:

Once there was a lake that changed colors three times a day.
A girl came and played there every day.
Her best friend came, too.
Then more friends came.
They played until it was time to go home for dinner.
They had chicken and french fries.

Thomas loved to make science books. He would staple several pieces of paper together, and then proceed to fill up the book. Sometimes he would draw an animal on each page and label it; sometimes he would list interesting facts he knew; sometimes he would copy information from animal cards or books.

For some seven- and eight-year-olds, writing becomes something you do in school and stops being play. For others, creative writing continues to be enjoyable. Eight-year-old Callie is writing her first chapter book, *Amy Anders and the Mystery of the Wild Goose Chase*. It's a mystery story, with two girl detectives as the heroines. But the story is as much about the relationship between the two girls, who argue, part with hurt feelings, make up, and decide to work together after all, as it is about solving the case. Callie's parents are intrigued by the way the arguments in the story mirror Callie's current difficulties with her best friend.

Books are just one kind of writing that five-to-eight-year-olds do. Children just learning to write may practice—just for fun—by copying book titles, writing their names, or making lists of family members. Some five- and six-year-olds still use pretend writing squiggles or random letters that look like writing and that only they can "read." Others ask parents to spell words for them when they want to write. Brittany, at seven,

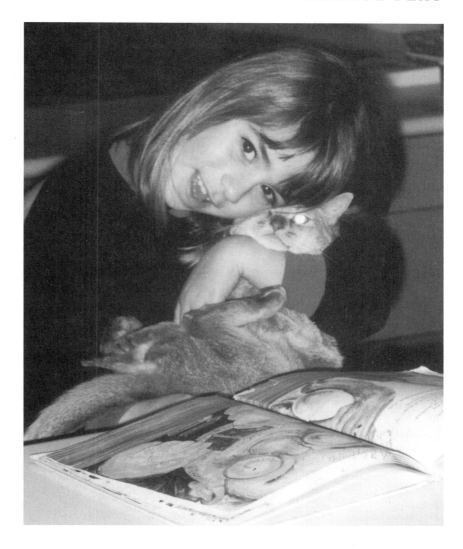

writes quite legibly but is not yet confident in either her reading or spelling. She loves to write notes to her Mom, such as "I want to watch TV" or "I want ice cream." Brittany asks her mother to spell each word, writes it down, and silently hands her mother the finished note.

Alice, at five, has not yet learned to read, but she can form most letters. She likes to write captions for her drawings and simple notes to family friends she hasn't seen and misses. "Dear Moose, We would like to see you soon. Love, Alice." Alice sometimes asks her mother to spell the words; sometimes she has her mother write the whole caption or note and then laboriously copies it.

Marissa at seven wrote in her diary every night. The diary was "private," but sometimes when Marissa got tired she'd ask her Mom to "write what I dictate but don't listen." Typical entries described her day, what she did and how it went. When she came to something that she thought really private, like how she felt about another person, Marissa would take over the writing.

Many children incorporate writing into their pretend play, making menus, grocery lists, theater tickets and programs, signs to keep intruders out of the clubhouse or to protect special possessions and creations, dog tags for their stuffed animals, report cards for their dolls, prescriptions for their human or animal patients, coded messages, treasure maps, cards, and invitations.

Children also like to use their emerging writing skills to help out in the family. Bobby made some signs when his new baby sister was born: "My mommy is breast feeding." "Shh. My baby is sleeping." Lisa stuck a piece of paper on the refrigerator and wrote "choklat chip cookys" when the family ran out. David used the computer to make his own invitations for his seventh birthday party.

Writing love notes is another activity that many children engage in and not only on Valentine's Day. "Dear, Mom," wrote Xavier, "I love you a lot. You are a gem to me." Angela makes picture books for her grandmother with a simple caption: "I love you." "Don't look in my pocket," Steven warned his mother. "I wrote a love note to Christy. I didn't give it to her because I thought the other children would make fun of me." Becky writes letters to imaginary friends, with whom she also converses on the phone. She also writes real letters to her aunt and enjoys receiving the replies. Karin is always writing letters, although most of them are never sent.

Seven-year-old Xavier loves to send and receive mail. He opens all the junk mail that arrives at his house, before anyone else can get it. If there's something you can send for, Xavier will fill out the form and send it in. His parents didn't mind too much when he ordered a complete set of Disney books. They were a little taken aback, though, when a letter came from Uncle Sam.

"Dear Xavier, We are glad that you are interested in joining the Navy. Please contact our recruiting office at your earliest convenience so that we can set up an appointment."

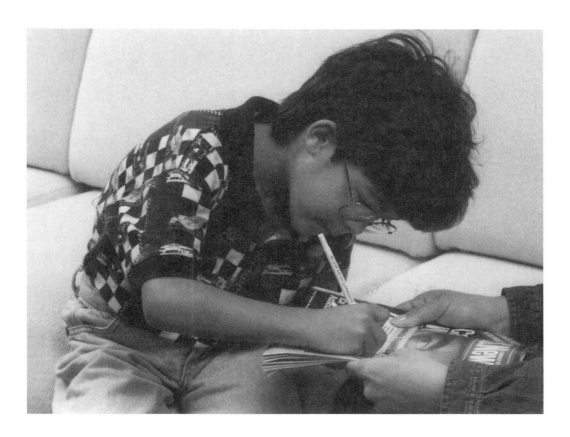

ARITHMETIC

"Hey, Mom," calls six-year-old Ethan. "Can you make me another sheet with math problems? Make them hard this time." Ethan is mathematically advanced, and also enjoys a challenge. His mother has taught him to "carry," and he likes to practice adding two-digit numbers.

Jessica, a home-schooled first grader, also likes to do "math papers," but she prefers story problems that challenge her to use her own strategies, such as figuring out how many cookies she would need to give everyone in her family three cookies. A problem like this can be approached in many ways—using fingers, poker chips, real cookies, paper and pencil, or mental math: counting out cookies one at a time until everyone has three, adding 3 + 3 + 3 + 3 + 3, counting by threes, or even taking a box of twenty cookies, giving everyone three, seeing how many are left, and subtracting or counting backwards. Jessica's mother encourages Jessica to explain the strategies she uses and to devise as many different ways of approaching a problem as she can. She also explains her own problem-solving strategies when they are different from Jessica's but within Jessica's grasp.

Five-year-old Becky likes to make up her own addition and subtraction problems, and write the problems and answers with magnetic letters on the refrigerator. She checks herself by counting on her fingers, or by using the magnetic letters as counters. Six-year-old Kevin also likes to show off his mathematical knowledge. He creates board games where the instructions about how many spaces to move are written as problems: go forward 3 + 2 spaces; go back 4 − 0 spaces.

Five-year-old Amy liked her mother to count to help her fall asleep. When counting by ones got too routine, they switched to counting backward, then counting by twos, fives, or tens, then counting by threes, fours, sixes, sevens, eights, or nines. With this early practice, Amy found it easy to master the multiplication tables and enjoyed being quizzed on the way to school.

Kori and Brenan, at eight and five, liked to play mental math games in the car. "What's twenty-seven plus thirty-three?" their mother would ask. "I know," said Kori. "Twenty-seven plus thirty is fifty-seven and three more is sixty." "I can do it a different way," said Brenan. "Twenty-seven plus three is thirty and thirty more is sixty." Benjamin, who has just turned five, is the youngest of three siblings. Like Kori and Brenan's family, Benjamin's family loves to quiz each other in the car. Benjamin is just beginning to grasp the idea of adding. "Supposing you have three cookies and I give you one more. How many cookies would you have?" his older sister asked. Benjamin counted on his fingers. "One-two-three-four." "What if you have three and I give you *two* more? How many would have then?" Benjamin counted on his fingers again, starting again at one. "One-two-three-four-five," he announced proudly.

Myles, at six, is very interested in money. His parents give him a small allowance, which he enjoys spending but especially likes to save. Every week, he dumps out his piggy bank and counts his money. With some help (and occasional interference) from his older sister, he has learned how to put the coins into piles of a dollar. He now knows what coins he needs to complete each pile. Every time he gets five dollars, he begs his parents to exchange it for a five-dollar bill. Now that he has six five-dollar bills, he considers himself exceedingly rich!

Arran's fascination is with large numbers. He combs through almanacs and the *Guinness Book of World Records,* and is constantly regaling his family with impressive statistics. He can tell you just how far away the moon is, or how long ago his favorite dinosaurs lived. Picking up on this interest, his father taught him the powers of ten. "One hundred is ten times ten, or ten to the second power. One thousand is ten times ten times ten, or ten to the third power." "I get it," said Arran. "You just count the zeros!" Arran enjoys telling people that he knows "high school math," and that the dinosaurs died out sixty-five times ten to the sixth years ago.

Caroline became fascinated with fractions when she realized that a quarter note in music, a quarter cup in a recipe, and the quarter in her pocket were all one fourth of a whole. She enjoys playing around with this concept as she doubles and triples recipes, writes her own songs, calculates her exact age, and figures out how to cut up and fairly distribute pizza, birthday cake, and brownies.

Nicky's entrée into higher mathematics, like his path into reading and writing, came through baseball. He got very interested in batting averages, and learned to compare them. Soon, he was wondering what an average was. His father showed him with simple numbers. Nicky, of course, then needed to work out his own batting average, with the help of a calculator.

Except in families where children or parents have particularly strong mathematical interests, most of the math play that children engage in is informal and incidental. Katie likes to play Monopoly with her older siblings and to borrow her big cousin's computer version. Since Katie usually prefers to let someone else do the math, her family was surprised one day when she complained, correctly, that she hadn't been given enough change. Kevin, by his own admission, is not so good at math problems involving money. "It's your fault, Mom," he explains. "You always use a credit card."

Like Katie, Fahran uses math to his advantage. When he and his mom go shopping, Fahran is always looking for bargains. "This Nintendo game costs thirty dollars, but we can get three games for eighty-five dollars and save five dollars." Once, when he had been given a gift of five dollars, Fahran managed to buy four small toys, with only eight cents left over. Adding up the prices in his head was a challenge, and he had to try several combinations of toys before he got close to five dollars without going over. He seemed to have as much fun with the math problem, though, as he did playing with the toys.

COLLECTING FACTS

Did you know that:

- Africa is the continent with the most countries?
- The Komodo dragon is the largest lizard in the world and it can run 35 miles an hour?
- Frogs and lizards are good to have around your house because they catch bugs?
- If you hold your nose and lick an onion it will taste sweet?
- Pluto is sometimes closer to the sun than Neptune, and may not have always been a planet?

These are just a few of the facts that we learned from our interviews with five-to-eight-year-olds and their parents.

Some children, like Justin, collect facts that they can incorporate into their play. Justin, who constantly plays at war games, is especially interested in speed, strength, and danger. He knows how fast a jet can fly or a jaguar can run; which carnivorous dinosaurs were the largest and what they ate; what weapons were used at different times in history.

Caroline also incorporates facts into her imaginative play, but her fact-collecting interests are most apparent in her stories. Historical facts are especially useful to her; she loves imitating the American Girl books she reads and adding accurate details of how people lived long ago or in different cultures to the stories and chapter books she writes. Jenna also studies different countries, both at home and at school. She uses the new information she learns to plan cruises for her Barbie dolls, figuring out just what they should eat, buy, and visit at each port of call.

Many children, like Arran, collect facts that are impressive. Whether it be Hank Aaron's home run record, the age of the Earth, or how much William Howard Taft weighed, Arran is always trying to find something startling that others don't know.

Other children, like Alice, want to keep up with what is going on around them. Five-year-old Alice lives with her parents and her ten-year-old sister, an avid reader with adult tastes and interests. The family frequently watches educational television or reads aloud from religious texts. Not wanting to be left out, Alice works hard to learn as much of what everyone else is learning as she can comprehend.

Children like Deanna like to learn a subject in depth. In first grade, Deanna read a children's book on the presidents. She was intrigued with both the trivia and the history, and practically memorized the book. Her teacher then suggested some children's biographies of famous women, which Deanna devoured with relish.

Alan knows all about rocks. He has a large rock collection, divided into igneous, sedimentary, and metamorphic sections, with each rock carefully labeled. His interest was sparked by a geologist who came to his school and helped the children identify the rocks they found on the playground.

Thomas is an expert on animals. He has large collections of realistic-looking rubber animals, *National Geographic* videos, *Zoobooks*, and nature magazines. Before he could read, he could identify almost any exotic animal and cite at least one interesting fact about it.

Lisa and Ethan exemplify a different style. For them, all facts are interesting. Given a choice of reading material, they often choose nonfiction. When the books don't supply enough information—and they usually don't—they ask for more. Children like these are always catching their parents off guard because they seem to know things that their parents swear they were never taught. Lisa gave a "dissertation on taste buds" as she and her mother made lemonade. Ethan, when asked by a teacher how many days there were in a month, explained that there were four answers: twenty-eight, twenty-nine, thirty, and thirty-one.

SCIENCE EXPERIMENTS AND INVENTIONS

Ned, an active seven-year-old, is constantly engaging in what he and his family call "science experiments." One day, his parents came downstairs and found balls of clay stuck to the windowpane. Immediately they recognized "the mark of Ned." The next day they discovered a sink filled with a mixture of water and milk. "What happens when I mix these things together?" Ned always seems to be asking. "What colors, textures, and patterns can I make? Can I make things soggy, or slimy, or sticky?" Cooking, especially baking, is a favorite activity. Ned loves to watch cookies rise in the oven, and see them change from gooey to crispy as they cool. Ned's favorite experiments involve placing one of his action figures in a pitcher of water, leaving it in the freezer for a few days, and then trying to chop the figure out of the ice.

Brittany, also seven, is another experimenter. She likes to make "magic potions" by mixing water with sand and dirt, sometimes sprinkling in flower petals or dried fir needles, sugar or salt, ice cubes or grape juice. Although much of the time she is merely pretending, Brittany also investigates floating and sinking, solution and precipitation, evaporation and condensation as she works with various concoctions.

Lisa's experiments are more formal. Right now, she is interested in electricity, perhaps because her neighborhood has experienced several recent power outages. Her parents gave her a batteries and bulbs set, and Lisa loves to set up different circuits and see if she can make the lights go on and off.

Fahran experiments in a different way. He likes to take things apart to see how they are put together and how they operate.

Steven, at six-and-a-half, is an inveterate inventor. He's always building something: a multipurpose tool, a weapon that shoots bullets and arrows at the same time, a miniature golf course for marbles, a trap for invisible barges. Often, the family will find toys tied together or odd assortments of objects carefully arranged in a pattern that they can't interpret—signs that their inventor has been at work.

Other children come up with ideas but don't actually make physical models. Katie, who loves to sleep in her mother's bed whenever her father is away, invented "sleep socks—so you can sleep with your mommy and her legs won't itch you." "You could sell them in the mall in the middle part and make money," Katie explained. Lisa invented a light that goes on in the shower when the house lights go off. Five-year-old Sarah, who is just learning to tell time, wants a "talking clock" so she won't have to worry about reading the numbers. Kevin plans to be a factory worker—"so I can make anything I need or want"—and also a scientist. "Save your money, Mom. I'm going to MIT." One of his first products will be a "flashlight that you can see through buildings with."

ANSWERS TO PARENTS' QUESTIONS

My child resists doing homework. What can I do about it?

While some children between five and eight are delighted to do homework, most children will do some procrastinating or resisting. In the preschool years they were free to spend at home time choosing their own activities. It is not easy to face the fact that there is work that has to be done on a regular basis that takes away from play. Parents are likely to be most successful if they establish a regular time for doing homework, either before or right after dinner. Children need to know that homework time is homework time. If they finish their work in less than the allotted time, then they are free to read a book or engage in another quiet activity. Once homework time has been set, it is important to keep to the schedule. The more lenient you are about changing or omitting homework time the more likely you are to get into hassles.

Should I help my child with her homework?

All parents want their children to do well in school, so it is natural to want to help a child with her homework. Answering questions about an assignment, quizzing your child if she requests it, or helping your child find a resource are legitimate ways of being helpful. It is also fine to encourage your child to check her work. Guard against pointing out specific errors that your child has made. Your child is likely to get careless if she knows you will point out her errors. Doing homework for a child or correcting her papers is not wise; the teacher can be more effective if she knows where your child needs help.

If your child has unusual difficulty with writing assignments, you may want to discuss with the teacher when it would be appropriate for her to dictate to you and when it would be better for her to write or type herself, even if she only produces a few words. When taking dictation, be sure not to change your child's words. Also, be sure that your child writes at least part of the assignment independently, so as not to lose out on valuable practice with writing, punctuation, and spelling.

Increasingly, schools are giving some homework assignments that are designed to foster home-school connections. You may be asked to share your own school experiences with your child, to create a diorama together, or to share an aspect of your family history or culture. Your participation is vital in assignments like these; take advantage of the opportunity to share with your child and don't worry about impressing the teacher.

My child isn't reading yet, though many of his classmates are. Are there playful things that I can do at home without making this a big issue?

You are wise to avoid making a big issue out of reading. Children learn to read at different times, just as they learn to walk at different times. By third grade most children have learned to read, even if they got a somewhat later start than other children. Fortunately there are many playful ways of encouraging your child to read without playing teacher. Let your child see that you and your spouse enjoy reading. Read good literature to your child so that he can develop a love of books. Write simple notes to your child and put them on the refrigerator or in his lunch box. Children need to know that reading is a useful skill. Read with your child, letting him read every other page, or letting him read the words he knows. Play word games with your child.

My child thinks he isn't "smart" because he isn't in the highest groups at school. What should I do?

Telling children that they really are smart when they have already established their own standard of smartness is not likely to work very well. Find out what children are in the same academic groups as your child and talk about how smart they are. If your child argues that the children you are talking about are not in the highest group, help your child understand that there are many ways of being smart and that not being placed in a particular reading or arithmetic group doesn't mean that you are not smart. Also, talk to the teacher about your child's perceptions. She may be able to give some group assignments that draw on your child's special strengths and to find ways to highlight his "smartness" for him and for his classmates. If your child is behind where he should be in a particular area, she may be able to give you some activities to do at home to strengthen his skills.

Our school doesn't give grades. How can I find out where my child stands in the group?

You are fortunate to have your child in a school that does not use letter grades. What you want to know is not what other children are doing but what your own child is doing. A report card that uses comments rather than letter grades gives you an opportunity to find out about your child's strengths and to learn about areas where your child's work needs improvement.

It is quite likely that your child will measure herself against her classmates on a number of dimensions. It doesn't really matter how accurate her perceptions are, as long as she feels good about herself and strives to do her best. Being at the top of the class in first grade is not a particularly good predictor of life success; what really matters is that your child continues to be curious, kind, and creative, as well as active, imaginative, and happily engaged in school.

When should I get my child tutored or tested?

It is not good to subject your child to an IQ test unless it is required for admission into a particular program. An IQ test will not tell you anything about your child that you do not already know. However, there are situations where an evaluation of your child may be valuable. Many types of learning disabilities and attention deficits can be detected early, at a time when remediation is most likely to be successful. If your classroom teacher recommends evaluation, take his advice. He is in a good position to know your child's problems as well as her strengths. If your child seems particularly frustrated and you are not sure why, testing may also be helpful. Have her vision and hearing checked before looking for possible learning problems.

Unless the teacher or a specialist recommends it, we do not advise having your child tutored in order to catch up with the class or with the top group. However, if your child has a special interest in which classes are not conveniently available, you might hire a tutor for her alone or for her and a friend. For example, if your child is interested in science, you may be able to find a high school or college student who can do experiments with her, take her to the library, and help her organize her collections into a science museum.

PLAY IDEAS

- Play a game with your child of finding little words hiding inside big ones. For example, there's a "tree" in "street," a "Nana" in "banana," a "kit" in "kite," and an "ape" in "newspaper." What other examples can your child discover?

- Some children enjoy reading in "secret" spaces, where no one can see or interrupt them. A wide windowsill with a curtain in front, a tree house, a mattress hidden behind a couch or bookshelf, a large box with windows cut out and a pillow inside, even a chair turned backwards—can be special, intimate spots for reading.

- Many schools have introduced "Sustained Silent Reading," a fifteen-minute period at the beginning or end of the day in which everybody reads. Your family might enjoy a similar family reading time at home. Nonreaders can participate by looking at picture books or making picture books to be shared with the family. You might want to also set aside some time for talking about what you are reading or sharing favorite passages.

- Keep some of your child's favorite "baby" books and picture books even when your child has moved on to chapter books. Occasionally read them together.
- Read aloud to or with your children. Include some books that you love, even if they are beyond their reading level and stretch their comprehension. Let each child read some passages or read the parts of some of the characters. Get books on tape for long car rides.
- Give your child a gift of a special blank book, to fill with poems, pictures, or special writings. Some families pass these books down from generation to generation. When given the book that had been her mother's, Kori wrote her first poem:

> *I like this book*
> *I like it a lot*
> *And I will pass it down to my*
> *Great great great great*
> *Great great great great grandchild*

- Post the shopping list on the refrigerator and let your children add items.
- Celebrate your child's ability to read independently with a special trip to the library to get your child her very own library card.
- Play commercial word games like Boggle, Scrabble, On-Words, UpWords, and Spill and Spell. Modify the rules so children can participate along with adults. You might have

adult-child teams, play open-handed and help each other, give children more credit for words than adults get, allow younger children to use shorter words, or allow invented spelling. Most children prefer the "real" game with appropriate accommodations to a children's version.

- Jotto is a strategic word game that can be played anywhere with paper and pencil. Good readers can learn it at seven or eight, and enjoy it into adulthood. Each player thinks of a secret five-letter word. Players try to guess each other's words by "testing" five-letter words to see how many letters of the opponent's secret word they contain. Each letter is counted individually; so, for example, if the secret word is "teeth," the test word "night" would contain two letters, H and T; the test word "eerie" would also contain two, the two E's. Generally, each player writes out the alphabet, crosses out letters that are definitely not in the opponent's word, and circles letters that are.

- Dictionary is a fun game to play with a large mixed-age group. One player looks in the dictionary, finds a word that she doesn't know, reads it aloud, and writes out its definition. Other players make up their own definitions, trying to make them sound plausible. The first player then reads out all of the definitions, giving each a number. Players record the number of the definition they think is correct. Players get one point for a correct guess and one point for each time their definition was guessed.

- A deck of cards can be used for a variety of math games. Go Fish, played with standard rules, helps young children practice recognizing and matching numbers. For children who are learning arithmetic facts, modify the rules so that a set consists of a problem and an answer, for example 3, 4, and 7 or 5, 8, and King. Casino also involves adding, as well as mental flexibility. Many children like to invent their own card games.

The plant grew so tall that it touched the clouds.
I climbed it and I touched the moon. A giant came
down and broke the Empire State Building in half.

• Encourage your child to dictate stories to go with his drawings. Write out his words or type them on a computer and
display them with his drawing.

- Keep a piggy bank. When it is full let your child help sort out the money according to denomination. If you have a lot of pennies, let your child make ten stacks of ten pennies and put them in coin wrappers. Go through a similar process with nickels, dimes, and quarters. When all your coins are wrapped, you and your child can go to the bank and change the coins to dollars.
- Start a family Spare Change Jar, and let children help count its contents. You might want to save up for a family goal, such as a special pizza party or a contribution to a charitable organization.
- Place some small objects or coins in one hand and some in the other. Tell your child how many (or how much money) you have all together. Then open one hand. Can your child figure out what the other hand contains? Let her take a turn to quiz you.
- If your children like playing store, let them use real coins and make play money for bills.
- Let your children play with money and practice making change. When learning to make change, most children find it easier to add than to subtract. For example, if an item cost $3.27, a child might figure: three cents more makes $3.30, then I need 70¢ to get to $4 and $1 more to get to $5, so from $5 you get $1.73 in change. Counting out real money, using, for example, pennies, then dimes, then dollars, will be easier than trying to do the problem mentally.
- Give your child a pile of pennies, nickels, and dimes. See if she can come up with three or four different ways of getting 25 cents.
- Play estimation games with your children. How many people are on the bus? What time will you arrive at your destination? How many red gumdrops are in the package? Let everyone guess, then count, and see who comes closest.
- Let your child help you figure out or estimate real problems, such as how much money you have spent, how much

change you should get, which item or package is the better buy, how to adapt a recipe to your family's needs, or how long it will take you to reach a destination on a long trip. Break the problem down, and help your child follow the strategies that you use to solve it. Ask her to solve the parts she can.

- Play "What's my rule?" Give three examples of pairs that are generated by a number rule, for example 2, 6; 4, 8; and 15, 19 all use the rule "add 4." See if your child can guess the rule from the examples. Can your child make a "What's my rule?" problem for you?

- Make up number riddles and challenge your children to make some up for you. For example, "I'm thinking of a number that's bigger than 10, but smaller than 20. If I add its digits together I get 3."

- If you have a computer, help your child use it to make greeting cards, invitations, signs, labels for collections, and items such as restaurant menus, play money, tickets, and secret codes to use in pretend play.

- Help your child make a "checkbook" to keep track of how he spends his allowance. Show him how to figure out how long it will take to save up for a special treat.

- Make Oobleck by mixing $1\frac{1}{2}$ cups of cornstarch and 1 cup of water to make soft dough.

    1. Pour the water into the bowl and slowly stir in the cornstarch.

    2. Slowly sink your hand into the bowl. "Grab" the soft dough and pull up.

    3. Roll the soft dough into a ball. You can add a bit of food coloring if you wish.

    Your child will enjoy experimenting with this unusual material which stretches, drips, squeaks, molds, bounces, and breaks. What happens when you add more cornstarch or more water? You might also read aloud the story that inspired its name: *Bartholomew and the Oobleck*, by Dr. Seuss.

- Make Silly Putty or Gak by mixing 1 cup liquid starch and 2 cups Elmer's glue (not "school glue"). Mix and work with hands until it hardens. You may add food coloring.

  The fun of Silly Putty is its consistency and versatility. You can change its shape as often as you want, pull it apart, make holes in it, or pound it, and it can always be put back together and shaped into a ball. Talk with your child about the special qualities of this material. How does it compare to the store-bought kind?

- Goop is another fun material. Children love to stretch Goop and create a variety of weird shapes.

  To make Goop, use 2 cups salt and ⅔ cup water. Mix and beat 3 to 4 minutes. Remove and quickly add 1 cup cornstarch and ½ cup cold water.

  Encourage your children to talk about how Goop feels. What happens when you stretch a ball sideways, or hold it by the top? Will Goop stick to a window?

- Soap bubbles are also interesting for budding scientists to explore. What shapes do they form? What happens when two or more come together? What colors do they show in the light? Can you make bubbles of different sizes? What happens to their shapes when you make them really big?

  To enhance bubble fun, try this activity. The night before, mix ⅓ cup tempera paint and ⅓ cup liquid detergent. Add water to make one quart, then pour the mixture into a shallow pan. The next morning have your child use a straw to blow a mountain of bubbles. (Make a pinhole in the straw to prevent your child from drinking the soap.) Can your child make the bubbles look like a honeycomb? How high can she get the mountain before it collapses? What happens to the shapes of the bubbles when the ones next to them pop?

- Save broken toys, clocks, and appliances that your child can take apart.
- Keep a scrap box of items your child can use for "inventions." This can include mystery objects and parts, string, drinking straws, gears and wheels, unsharpened pencils, brass fasteners, tape, index cards, bubble wrap, aluminum foil, nuts and bolts, plastic containers, and other recycled materials.
- Make special places for your child's collections. If she shows interest, help her identify, organize, and label her treasures.
- Help your child make a museum on a shelf or in shallow drawers or shoe boxes. Its theme can be science, geography, history, art, dolls or toys, baseball cards, or anything that your child collects. Items should be carefully organized, displayed, and labeled. Your child may also want to write a short description.

CHAPTER 8

Family

~~~~~~~~~~~~~~~~~~~~~~~~~~~~~~~~

"Let's play change artist," Bobby suggested to his family. "You stay here and I'll go in my room and I'll change something on me. When I come back you have to guess what I changed." Bobby ran to his room, and came back with his jeans on backwards. "Can you guess what I changed?" Bobby asked. "I know," his father answered, "you painted your tongue green and orange." "No way," Bobby laughed, sticking out his tongue

to prove the point. After a few more preposterous guesses, his mother guessed right. "Your jeans are on backwards, the zipper is in the back!" "You got it," Bobby admitted, and ran back in his room to make another change.

Although Bobby's change artist game was his own unique invention, all children between five and eight years old are likely to be change artists. At one moment they amaze their family with their new sophisticated ideas and their insistence on not being babied. At the next moment they let their parents know they are not ready to grow up quite yet and want to stay close to home.

~~~

In this chapter we discuss issues of attachment and separation, children's parent-management techniques, and the building and maintenance of family continuity and traditions.

ATTACHMENT AND SEPARATION

"Mommy, I have a great idea," Alice announced as she and her mother walked the three blocks to kindergarten. "You could stay at my kindergarten with me, and we could have lots of fun." As Alice and her mother continued their three-block walk, Alice came up with a series of delaying techniques. "Mom, look! There's a beautiful butterfly. Let's chase it." "Mom, I know I can jump over the puddle. Let me try one more time." "Mom, let's go home and get our umbrella. I think maybe it's going to rain." Whether or not a child has had experience with preschool, the transition into elementary school can be major. Real school for young children represents a break from parents and a scary step into a big children's world where there are new teachers and new expectations.

Children like Alice who are hesitant to leave their parents are not necessarily immature. Five to eight years old is a time of transition. Children are striving to be more independent, to assume more responsibilities, but at the same time they want to hold on to the feeling of security provided by their family. The more opportunities children have to be on their own and encounter new experiences, the more they recognize how much they love to be safely at home with their parents.

Bobby is a prime example of a socially well-adjusted child who did not want to leave his mother. When Bobby's girlfriend, Katie, invited him to come over to their house for a sleepover, Bobby asked his mother if she would sleep over, too. When his friend from next door asked him to come over and play, Bobby's mother found him sitting in the kitchen with tears streaming down his face. "What's the matter?" she asked. "Christopher wants me to go and play at his house and I really want to go, but I also want to stay here with you." "Why don't you go and play with Christopher for a while and then come back home," his mother suggested. "I have a better idea," Bobby countered. "Why don't you come to Christopher's house with me and we can all play together."

Becky, like Bobby, had difficulty leaving her parents, especially at night. One night she got very brave and agreed to spend the night at a girlfriend's house. At ten o'clock her parents got the expected call. "Hi, Dad, this is Becky. I am just calling to make sure you and Mom are all right." Once she had checked in with her parents, Becky got up her courage and stayed at her friend's house all night.

Children who are very attached to their parents and who do not want to be separated are likely to worry about growing up and leaving their parents home. "I am going to marry my mommy," Benjamin told his friend. "Can I stay with you even if I'm married?" Katie asked her mother. "When I grow up," Kevin announced, "I am going to have a thousand wives, and I'll bring them back home to live."

While some children are concerned about growing up because they might have to leave home, other children associate growing up with the potential loss of a parent. "When I grow up and get old, will you still be alive?" Bobby asked his father. "We can't give Daddy any more birthday parties," Ned insisted, "'cause I don't want him to grow old and die."

Many children are fearful not only about losing a parent through death but also about losing a parent through divorce. Kate was friendly with some schoolmates who belong to the "Banana Split Club," a special support group for children whose parents had separated. After she heard about the club, Kate was concerned when her parents had even the mildest disagreement. "Stop screaming at each other," she insisted, as she planted herself between her parents. Like Kate, Leigh got upset when her parents had an argument. "Do parents who are married stop loving each other?" she asked in a worried voice.

Sarah's parents separated when she was still an infant, and Sarah had a different take on divorce. When she and her mother were at a restaurant, the couple at the next table started quarreling with each other. "Why don't they get a divorce?" Sarah asked, in a voice that was much too loud.

While some children fret over divorce when their parents argue, many children also feel jealous and threatened when their parents pay attention to each other. Katie insisted on lying on the bed between her mother and father so they wouldn't get too close to each other. Phoebe got angry when her parents danced with each other at a family reunion. Kate felt put out when her mother and father kissed each other on the lips. Darryl complained about his mother and father being so "kissy and huggy." At the same time he was terribly afraid that something bad would happen to his family. When his father announced that he was going across the street to visit a neighbor, Darryl told his father to be careful to watch out for cars. When his mother climbed on a stepladder to reach for a dish, he told her to get down immediately. "Don't you know," he scolded, "ladders are dangerous."

Natural disasters such as hurricanes, earthquakes, or tornadoes can exacerbate a child's fear of separation. Marvin's father, who was a policeman, stayed away for two days during Hurricane Andrew. Any mention of a hurricane on television, even if it was on the other side of the world, put Marvin into a panic. Jeremy, who lived in California, was afraid of floods and earthquakes. Jeremy begged his father to build a big tree house in the backyard. "Then I won't be scared anymore 'cause we can all move to my tree house."

In families with more than one child, children are attached to each other as well as their parents. No matter how much they quarrel with a sibling, they also feel connected. When Arran's sister Kori left for college, she worried that he would feel bereft. She gave him two of her favorite stuffed animals and asked him to take very good care of them, which he did. Arran had his school picture blown up to "wall size" so she could put it up in her room. When Katie's big brother left, she and her sister secretly packed his favorite stuffed animal in his suitcase. They knew that he really wanted to take it along, but was afraid to say so. Pesky little sisters can be a very useful excuse.

As we watch children struggle with the threat of separation, we recognize how ambivalent children feel about growing up. On the one hand children are saying to their parents, "I want to go out and be with my friends and I don't want you to stop me." On the other hand they are saying, "I need you very badly and I want you to be with me all the time and forever."

When young children are immersed in the struggle between gaining independence and remaining dependent, they are likely to behave in ways that are sometimes difficult to deal with and sometimes most endearing.

PARENT-MANAGEMENT TECHNIQUES

Parents who describe their five-to-eight-year-olds as being delightful to live with very often follow a string of positive adjectives with a "but." Angela is described by her mother as sweet, dynamic, self-motivated, and a friendly child, "but" she blocks you out and pays no attention when she doesn't want to do what you say. Mark is described as friendly, wanting to please, and full of fun, "but" he is persistent, headstrong, and always wants his own way. James is described as highly motivated, friendly, and creative, "but" he is not a good listener and is stubborn and impossible to redirect.

No matter how many parents we interview, the "buts" all point to the same emerging characteristics. Children between five and eight want to take charge, to discard parental directions, and do things their own way. The techniques children use to accomplish these objectives include pleading, manipulating, negotiating, and teasing. Children also attempt to keep their parents in a good mood by using flattery, empathy, and endearing terms and by demonstrating remorse when they offend.

Pleading

One of the most common techniques that children use to get what they want is nonstop pleading. By the age of five, many children are proficient and persistent pleaders. "Please, Mommy, just one more cookie. I really need it." "Daddy had a second dessert, so why can't I?" "I just got to do it one more time." These kinds of pleas resonate with most parents. After a while many parents give in, which of course reinforces the pleading.

Benjamin pleaded with his mother to buy some candy as they stood in line at the supermarket. His mother decided that she did not want him to make a scene. Knowing that he hated gumdrops, his mother let him choose between a bag of gumdrops or a box of raisins. As expected, Benjamin chose the raisins and was perfectly content.

When they got into the car, Benjamin refused to put on his seat belt. "Please, Mommy, don't make me wear a seat belt. It hurts my tummy real bad." "You don't have a choice about seat belts," his mother insisted. "But just this one time," Benjamin pleaded. "I can start the car just as soon as your seat belt is done up," his mother responded firmly. Recognizing that this time his mother meant business, Benjamin put on his seat belt. Benjamin's mother had learned the hard way that you either agree to compromise on the first request or you don't compromise at all. At the same time, Benjamin realized that nonstop pleading would not increase his chances of getting his way.

While children may give up persistent pleading, bargaining, negotiating, and manipulating are less likely to go away. The most common type of bargaining is the "if-then" variety. "If you buy me just one little car, I won't ask you to get me one more thing." "If you let me watch television for just five more minutes, I promise you I'll sit right down and do my homework."

Katie is particularly good at manipulating her mother. When her mother has people over and she wants her attention, she will tell her mother that she is tired and wants to go to bed. Her mother leaves her friends and goes upstairs with her. Once in bed, Katie likes to prolong her nighttime rituals. She asks her mother for a drink of water and then instructs her mother on how she wants to drink it. "If I say 'wheedle'," she tells her mother, "that means I want to sit up and have a little sip of water." "If I say 'Cuby Doll,' that means I want to sit up and have a big gulp of water."

When Becky wants her way about something, her favorite technique is negotiation. "Mommy, please may I have five pieces of candy?" "Five pieces? You know you can't have candy before dinner." "How about four pieces?" "Absolutely not. Candy is bad for your teeth." "Well, then, I'll settle for two pieces." Tired of arguing, her mother gives in and offers a compromise. "Okay, you can have one piece of candy and that's all."

Other negotiators prepare the ground with a touch of charm or flattery. Darryl promised his mother that if she would just let him watch the rest of the television show, he would be her best friend. Leigh paved the way for making a confession by telling her mother how nice it was that she could talk to her, knowing she would always listen.

Jessica loves to be read to, especially during mealtimes. Her mother feels that it is time to wean Jessica from her pattern of needing to be read to while eating. But Jessica is a master negotiator: "If you read to me while I eat lunch, I'll drink my milk," she'll say one day. The next day she'll try a new tack: "You can sit on the couch where it's comfortable. I'll still be able to hear you."

Brittany, who had had difficulty learning to write, used her newfound skills to get her mother to comply with her requests. One morning her mother found the following note attached to the refrigerator. "Mommy, will you buy me a Beanie Baby?"

Endearing Ways

While five-to-eight-year-olds can wear parents down with non-stop bargaining and pleading, they can also surprise them with shows of empathy and tact. When Jack's mother dropped a frozen food package on her toe, Jack responded with genuine empathy. "Oh, Mom, are you all right? Did you hurt yourself?" When Brittany's mother served a salad of raw vegetables, Brittany took one bite of her broccoli, pushed the plate away, and said politely to her mother, "Mom, you cooked this dinner very well, but next time would you cook the vegetables a little bit longer?" Bobby's mother had just given birth to a baby girl. "Mommy," said Bobby in his sweetest voice, "I like the size you are now, but when are you getting back to your real size?" When Katie's mother expressed her concern about gaining weight, Katie reassured her, "You are not fat, Mommy, you are just a little bit F.A.T." These six-year-olds were in tune with their mothers' feelings and knew just how to make them smile.

The flip side of wanting to please parents is not wanting to displease them. Alan was worried because he lied to his mother about brushing his teeth right before Yom Kippur. "Mother, can I have your forgiveness?" he pleaded. Jenna's parents heard her sobbing in her room after they had put her to bed. They returned to her room to find out what the problem was. Jenna blurted out, "Me and my friend wrote our names on the wall and my conscience is hurting!"

FAMILY CONTINUITY AND TRADITIONS

Although parents are the most important people in their children's world, grandparents in many families run a close second. In some families children think of their grandparents as "pushovers." Darryl and Devon decided that they wanted a tent for the backyard. "I think it's expensive," Darryl told his brother. "Do you suppose we better ask Grandpa?" For other children, grandparents are auxiliary parents who are automatically on-call whenever their parents can't be with them. Bobby's mother was worried because she couldn't be at her son's first grade performance. "No problem," Bobby assured her. "Nanny and Poppy would love to come and watch me."

In addition to being gift givers, playmates, or best boosters, grandparents are the repository of family tradition. They help children know not only who they are, but where they come from. Fahran's family is from India. When his grandmother comes to visit, dressed in her native clothes and speaking a language that Fahran does not understand, there is an immediate bond between grandson and grandmother. As he sits beside her at the table, he bows his head when she says grace and wipes his lips with his napkin when he sees her wipe her lips. After dinner he sits beside his grandmother in front of the fireplace, and the two of them are silent as they look through a photo album that she brought over from India.

Xavier's family also works hard to maintain family ties. Twice a year they visit Xavier's father's family in Mexico and his maternal grandparents in Peru. Xavier's parents speak only Spanish in their home so that Xavier and his sister will feel at home when they make their yearly visits.

Holidays and celebrations provide special opportunities for families to get together, and carry on family traditions. Christmas, for Darryl and his family, is more than a time to get presents from Santa. Every year, two weeks before Christmas, Darryl goes Christmas shopping with his grandfather. One Christmas as they worked their way through the shopping list, Darryl and his grandfather discussed each member of the family. "We have to buy a gift for your cousin, Pierre. What do you think he'd like?" "Well, last year when he came for Christmas he brought his baseball cards, and we played with them

together. Maybe he would like some football cards this year, and then we could play again."

Katie's family often gets together for her nana's birthday. Sometimes the family crowds into nana's house; for special birthdays they all take a trip together. The cousins have started a tradition of their own: they bought their nana a dollhouse and help to keep it stocked. For every birthday, the children search for special accessories that reflect their personalities. Greg buys the desserts, Tom makes sure that the pets have food and toys, Kori is concerned about playground equipment, Caroline has contributed the piano, phonograph, and violin, and Katie is in charge of the babies.

Mark is from a large extended family who live in the same town. For them, Passover is an especially important celebration. Every year a different family takes a turn hosting the

Passover Seder. No matter whose house they are in, Mark's grandfather sits at the head of the table and leads the Seder service. Everyone takes part in the service, dipping bitter herbs in salt water, eating matzo with haroses (an apple and nut mix), reciting the Pesach blessings, sipping wine, and searching for the Afikoman (a special piece of matzo hidden by the leader of the service, which the children hunt for and then exchange for a prize). The best part of the whole service, from Mark's point of view, is opening the door for the prophet Elijah. Elijah's cup of wine is set in the middle and the children expect invisible Elijah to come in and drink the wine. One day the neighbor's dog came into the dining room when they opened the door. Every year, when it's time to open the door for Elijah, the family retells the story of the dog's unexpected visit.

Even when there are no grandparents on call, families find many ways of preserving family traditions. Parents share their own childhood memories, show their children old photos, establish their own rituals and traditions, and tell and retell favorite family stories.

Crystal and her siblings love to hear their father tell stories about when he was a boy living on a farm. Their father describes the fun he had with his brothers climbing the apple trees, leaping from stone to stone to get across the creek, and riding the tractor into the gully and through the brush. The children especially love hearing about the day their father tried to climb the barbed-wire fence, got stuck on a barb, and had to run all the way home without his trousers on. Best of all, Crystal, the youngest, loves to look in the family album and find pictures of the farm. "I'm going to be a farmer when I grow up," she told her father.

Arran's father had lost both parents by the time Arran was born. His father and uncles kept alive a family tradition started by their father by telling their own children stories about the "Bald-Headed Chicken." Neither Arran's dad nor his dad's

brothers remembered these stories very well, so each reinvented them in his own way. When the cousins got together, they laughed at their fathers' different interpretations of the character their grandfather invented.

With or without intergenerational input, many families establish special rituals and traditions. Benjamin, Cara, and Jake's mother invented a series of family games that they would play at night as they sat around the kitchen table. "Choose a letter" was one of their favorite games. Each family member was given a turn choosing a letter of the alphabet and thinking of an object in the room that began with that letter. The point of the game was to think of an object that no one else in the room could guess. Benjamin chose the letter C. The family shouted out C words in rapid succession: Coke, catsup, cupboard, coffee maker, can opener, cookie jar. Finally, everyone gave up. Benjamin laughed triumphantly. "It's cucumber. We have cucumber mixed in our salad!"

Camellia's favorite holiday is Kwanzaa, a seven-day African-American holiday that emphasizes the values of sharing, faith, and community. During the holiday, Camellia and her mother bake special holiday cookies and bring some to the hospital for children who are sick.

Bedtime rituals are routine in many families. In Bobby's family, the children's favorite bedtime ritual is listening to their mother read a story. Even though Bobby and his brother are quite capable of reading on their own, a story read by their mother is always a special treat. When Mother finishes reading the story, Bobby's father comes into the bedroom and kisses the boys goodnight. He never forgets to give Bobby's teddy bear the very last good-night kiss.

In many of the families we spoke with, vacations were the time to create or continue family traditions. Endre's family has a family reunion every third year. There were at least seventy-five people at the last one, "so many people we couldn't even fit in the same McDonald's," Endre informed us. The families have lunch and dinner together, with each family taking a turn preparing the meal. After meals the children provide the entertainment. "I'm the best one at singing songs," Endre explained, "because I have the loudest voice."

In Alan and Jeff's family, summer trips have also become a tradition, and a new sightseeing journey is planned each year. The most important part of the trip, from the point of view of the children, is collecting neat things at each spot and putting them in a trip box as soon as they get home. Alan showed us some of the treasures from his last cross-country excursion: a snail shell, a ticket stub from the chairlift ride, a collection of paper placemats from fast-food restaurants, postcards, brochures, several rocks, a big bird eggshell, and several laundromat receipts. According to their mother, Alan and his brother spend hours taking the items out of the box and replaying each vacation.

For Sonia and Marissa, the fun of a vacation is following tradition. They go to the same spots each year, see the same friends and relatives, play the same board and card games, eat out in the same fast food restaurants, and visit the same parks. Without all of these components, as far as the girls are concerned, the vacation doesn't count.

While vacations provide a special opportunity for families to play together and create their own traditions, family fun is not limited to vacations. A very special way of having fun is telling family stories and sharing family jokes. Many families joke about their child's early attempts to master new words and phrases. James's family loved James's description of Robin Hood as "taking from the rich and giving to the porridge." No matter how many times his big sister corrected him, James continued to say, "Taking from the rich and giving to the porridge." Darryl had a similar problem with the Pledge of Allegiance. He inevitably began with "I pledge Alicia to the flag" (Alicia is his sister). Benjamin's family would never let him forget that he used to call spaghetti "psgetti."

Many family stories describe some silly thing their child did when she was little. Angela's family never forgot the day when she opened the refrigerator, took out an egg, put it on the floor and sat on it. When her father came into the kitchen, she asked him to be very quiet while she hatched her egg. Mark's family recalls the day when Mark insisted on putting his own new pajamas on his teddy bear. When his mother suggested that they were a little bit too big, Mark explained that he was just "tenting" his bear.

Another source of family stories are children's unusual sayings. When Lisa was just two and a half she told her parents, "I love Mommy and I love Daddy and I love butter." Bobby looked at a school of crabs crawling on the beach and announced that they were having a convention. Jenna had heard her grandmother use the expression "she's a'rearin'," to mean "she's acting up." One day Jenna picked up a wiggly newt and showed it to her mother. "Look, Mom," she exclaimed, "I think my newt is a'rearin'."

Some of the children and families we talked with had created a private language. When Brittany says "Beebah," her family has to guess from her tone of voice whether she means "Pay attention to me, now!" or "I refuse!" or "I like you." Caroline's family invented special nicknames used only within the family: Caroline was "Bean," her brother Tom was "Muffin," Greg was "Weggers," and Nick was "Nickelodeon." Arran's family serves "Sunday Night Smorgasbord" (leftovers), "Butter Milk" (a home remedy for sore throats), and "Mother-Special Eggs" (soft-boiled eggs fixed according to Arran's grandmother's recipe). Alan's family encourages each other to try new things by saying, "It's like the canoe," a reference to the day that Alan screamed in fear when his family tried to coax him into a canoe and then, once he decided to try it, screamed with delight as he paddled as fast as he could.

In Crystal, Janelle, and Richard's family, weekly rituals include a family outing, a Sunday barbecue, and two ball games, since both parents are coaches. Xavier's family has started a tradition of Sunday brunch. Xavier's father names a few restaurants that fit into their budget and the whole family, including Xavier's three-year-old sister, votes for their choice of restaurant.

As we look at the different ways in which families have fun together, we recognize that play is an important way to strengthen family ties. Parents who are playful with their children can manage out-of-line behavior without creating distance or power struggles. Parents who encourage and join in their child's play and who create a climate at home that allows play to flourish enhance the fun of daily living and provide their child with a skill that will not lose its value.

Caroline's father is the epitome of a playful parent. His sense of humor is contagious and he has an uncanny way of

using his humor to stifle troublesome behavior before it gets out of hand. When his four children get rambunctious on a car ride, he announces a contest. "Whoever can make the quietest noise wins the contest." For several seconds there is a dead silence. "I didn't tell you to be quiet, I told you to make the quietest noise." At this point the children try out whispers, whistles, hiccups, and sniffles. Of course no one gets to win the contest, but the children have so much fun with their quiet noises that the "out-of-hand" behavior is replaced with laughter.

Sonia and Marissa's mother has also discovered the power of playful parenting. When the children tracked mud into the house, she took out the vacuum cleaner and vacuumed each child with exaggerated motions. "Hmm, I guess I better vacuum your fingers, the back of your neck, under your arms, and now let's see, do you have some dirt piled up behind your ears?" The children giggled, took off their shoes, and enlightened their mother as to the source of the mud. Pretty soon, everyone was helping with the cleanup and no noses were out of joint.

Another way that parents encourage play is by joining in. When Caroline and Katie were playing Easy Street Restaurant, their mother played the part of customer. "This roll is delicious, but the soup is a little bit cold." "Don't worry, we'll warm it right up for you," Katie, the waitress, promised. "Ouch, now it's too hot. I just burned my tongue." Waitress Caroline promised to bring out a pitcher of ice cubes. The restaurant play continued until Caroline's mother paid the bill and went into the kitchen to make a real dinner.

In contrast to Caroline's mother, who joined her daughter's play, many parents shared their own play interests with their child. Caroline's father encouraged his children to share his passion for sports by inventing elaborate trivia and "betting" games that they played together as they watched big games on TV or discussed the predictions in the sports pages. Jessica's mother taught her to sew, and together they made a collection of simple stuffed dolls and animals. Darryl's father taught Darryl and a friend how to build a snow fort; Becky's mother invited her daughter to help her assemble a bookcase; Mark's father introduced his son to the wonders of ancient Egypt.

Some ways of encouraging play do not require active parent supervision. Kate's mother invited a playmate to the house and arranged a cookie-decorating activity. James's mother brought her son to the corner park and watched from a distance as he played. Sonia and Marissa's mothers created a child-centered house where play structures and miniature scenes were always left out, inviting children to play.

Children between five and eight are going through a very special time. Their peer group is of prime importance, and they welcome any opportunity to play with friends. At the same time, they are very attached to their family, and playing with parents is a special treat. As you play along with your children, you will continue to discover their talents, sense of humor, and emerging insights. You will appreciate more than ever their enthusiasm, imagination, and creative spirit.

ANSWERS TO PARENTS' QUESTIONS

How can I help my child develop a conscience?

Somewhere between five and eight years old most children develop a conscience. They are internalizing standards of right and wrong and feel badly when they violate their own standards. You can encourage this development by talking about instances after the fact where your child behaved in an appropriate way of his own accord without adult direction.

How can I increase my child's sensitivity to others?

Children learn by example. As your children see you express empathy and behave toward others in a nonjudgmental way, they increase their awareness of others' feelings and perspectives. Reading books to children, taking them to movies that describe caring children, providing children with animals to take care of, and giving your children an opportunity to interact with babies also encourage the development of empathy and responsibility.

If cheating is normal in five-year-olds, does that mean I should ignore it?

While it is important not to shame a child for cheating, it is quite appropriate to let the child know that you are aware of her strategy. You may want to say that a part of the fun of playing a game is giving everybody a fair chance to win. "Next time, let's see if we can play with no cheating tricks like counting wrong or putting the dice down instead of throwing it."

If I suspect that my child is lying to me, what is the best way to handle it?

Resist the tendency to ask your child whether she is lying or telling the truth. You are putting her in a situation where the best way of gaining your approval is to stand by her lie. If you don't know whether or not your child is lying, wait. The truth will out. If you are quite positive that your child is lying, make it clear to her that you know the truth and talk to her about her reasons for lying. Did she feel badly about what she did? Was she concerned about being punished? Was she trying to keep a friend out of trouble? If you talk to your child in a non-punitive way, she is more likely to tell the truth in another situation.

What do I do when my child is rude or demanding?

It doesn't usually work too well to scold your child for being rude or demanding. He is likely to deny it, and you may find yourself in a power struggle. In this situation a touch of humor goes a long way. "Your voice is hurting my ears. I understand you better when we just talk to each other." If your child continues to demand, you may want to say, "I said 'no' to you very clearly, and making unpleasant noises is not going to change my mind."

When should I give my children an allowance?

Opinions differ on allowances. Some families feel that children should be given an allowance so that they can learn about spending money wisely. Some families feel that allowance is something that you should earn. In still other families, the rules about money are more relaxed. Children are given money as needed for expenditures such as school lunch or special activities and for extras like books, healthy snacks, and presents for others. Although there are no hard-and-fast rules, families should not be much more liberal or much more restrictive than families of other children in the peer group. If your decision is to give your child an allowance, wait until he understands basic money concepts.

How do other people raise their children? What differences in values among families are you most likely to encounter?

Parents differ in their child-rearing beliefs on many

dimensions. Some dimensions are related to culture, some to family tradition, and some to individual differences among families. A traditional way of describing parents' child-rearing styles is *authoritarian,* where the parents make the rules, *authoritative,* where the parents set the standards but allow the children to participate in decision making, and *laissez-faire,* where the parents allow the children to set up the rules and create the standards. Other dimensions of difference described in the literature include the amount of parent warmth, the level of child-centeredness, and the degree to which independence and family obligations are stressed.

How do I teach my child about other cultures and religions?

Children learn best by real-life experiences. In your choice of schools, camps, neighborhoods, and after-school activities, seek out ways of exposing your children to a range of religions and cultures. Choose family friends from different religions and cultures and make a practice of going to each other's homes and sharing family traditions. Use vacations as an opportunity to visit places where you and your children will learn about different lifestyles. Take your children to different places of worship where they will learn about different religions. Attend festivals, fairs, and concerts and visit museums that will spark your child's interest in different forms of art. Encourage your children to ask questions about different life styles and answer the questions in a way that is meaningful to your children.

What can parents do to strengthen the relationships among their children, not just now but for the future?

All parents want their children to get along with each other. Constant quarreling among siblings is tiresome and annoying, but it is more than that. The dream of every parent is that their children will grow up to be good friends. When children quarrel all the time, parents become convinced that they never will like each other. In actuality, siblings who fought as children can be the best of friends as adults, laughing together about their childhood antics and quarrels. Creating opportunities for cooperation is the most surefire way of enhancing sibling relationships. Find projects that children can do together: making dinner for the family, packing for a camping trip, volunteering in a community project or helping out at a school or charity fair, buying holiday gifts for other members of the family, preparing a birthday surprise. At the same time, try to avoid situations that are likely to cause hard feelings, and be sensitive to situations where your attention can escalate a quarrel.

PLAY IDEAS

- Use humorous words to change your child's sulky mood, such as "Puppy Face," "Grumpy," or "Poor Eeyore." Be sure to say them in an exaggerated and gentle way, so that your child feels jollied rather than teased or picked on.
- Use a Simon Says game to encourage your child's rapid compliance with routines, such as getting dressed or clearing the table.
- Arrange play dates for each child with you and with your spouse. Give the days special names: "Buddy Days," "Children's Days," "Choice Days," "Good-Time Days," "Unbirthdays."
- Provide your children with experiences that make them aware of their family roots. You might share family stories, spend time with older relatives, trace the family's journey on a map, visit places where members of the family have lived, or organize family reunions.
- When your parents visit, ask them to tell the children about the music and dances that were popular when they were young, about the games they used to play, and about the places that they went to on vacation.

- Go through old albums and show your children pictures of their parents, grandparents, and great-grandparents. Talk about the clothes they were wearing, the homes they lived in, the kinds of cars they drove, and the chores and recreational activities they engaged in.
- If your children's grandparents came from a different place, use the Internet or the library to find photos and descriptions of their hometown or home country.
- Help your children make a simple family tree.
- Bring your children back to the places you knew and loved when you were a child.
- Continue to establish family traditions. Use holidays, vacations, and weekends to initiate new rituals that your children will enjoy and remember.
- Let your child help you create a family scrapbook that includes pictures, drawings, writings, and artifacts that have had meaning for your family. Include such things as school pictures, buttons, playbills, newspaper clippings, pressed flowers, embroidery yarn, or any other items that have meaning for your family.
- Choose books for your children to read that describe different kinds of families, different homes, and different cultures.
- Let your children help you write a family biography.

Recommended Reading

BOOKS FOR PARENTS

How to Talk So Kids Will Listen and Listen So Kids Will Talk, by Adele Faber and Elaine Mazlish. Illustrated by Kimberly Ann Coe (Avon Books)

Dragon Mom: Confessions of a Child Development Expert, by Janet Gonzalez-Mena (out of print, but a great book for parents who sometimes find their usually delightful five-to-eight-year-olds exasperating)

Raising Your Spirited Child: A Guide for Parents Whose Child Is More Intense, Sensitive, Perceptive, Persistent, and Energetic, by Mary Sheedy Kurcinka (Harper Perennial Library)

Raising Cain: Protecting the Emotional Life of Boys, by Daniel J. Kindlon and Michael Thompson (Ballantine Books)

Siblings Without Rivalry: How to Help Your Children Live Together So You Can Live Too, by Adele Faber and Elaine Mazlish (Avon Books)

Family Fun Activities

Playwise: 365 Fun-Filled Activities for Building Character, Conscience, and Emotional Intelligence in Children, by Denise Chapman Weston and Mark S. Weston (Putnam Publishing Group)

365 TV-Free Activities to Do with Your Child, by Steven J. Bennett and Ruth Bennett (Adams Media Corporation)

The Cooperative Sports and Games Book: Challenge without Competition, by Terry Orlick (Random House)

Let's Make a Memory: Great Ideas for Building Family Traditions and Togetherness, by Gloria Gaither, Shirley Dobson, and Russ Flint (Word Books)

SHARING READING WITH CHILDREN

Reading together is a wonderful way to share special moments with your child, to pass on values, to develop a common language for issues, feelings, and everyday situations, and to elicit your child's questions, concerns, and ideas. The following is a list of some of our favorite children's books that elaborate the themes of our chapters and capture the humor, wonder, serious struggles, and playful creativity of the years from five to eight. Because many five-to-eight-year-olds love following directions, we have also included collections of science experiments and simple craft and cookbooks that children can enjoy with adult support.

INDIVIDUAL DIFFERENCES AND COMMON THREADS

For Parents and Children Together

Daydreamers, by Eloise Greenfield. Illustrated by Tom Feelings (E. P. Dutton)

Free to Be You and Me: And Free to Be a Family, by Marlo Thomas. Edited by Christopher Cerf and designed by Barbara Cohen (Running Press)

Ramona the Pest, by Beverly Cleary (Camelot)

Stand for Children, by Marian Wright Edelman. Illustrated by Adrienne Yorinks (Hyperion Press)

Be Good to Eddie Lee, by Virginia Fleming. Illustrated by Floyd Cooper (Philomel Books)

Knots on a Counting Rope, by Bill Martin, Jr., and John Archembault. Illustrated by Ted Rand (Owlet)

For Beginning Readers

My Book about Me, By Me Myself, by Dr. Seuss and Roy McKie (Random House)

For Independent Readers

Everybody Cooks Rice, by Norah Dooley. Illustrated by Peter J. Thornton (Carolrhoda Books)

THE QUESTIONS CHILDREN ASK

For Parents and Children Together

Just So Stories, by Rudyard Kipling

Many Moons, by James Thurber. Illustrated by Marc Simont (Harcourt, Brace, Jovanovich)

One Morning in Maine, by Robert McCloskey (Puffin Books)

How You Were Born, by Joanna Cole. Photos by Margaret Miller (William Morrow and Co.)

I Wonder Why Soap Makes Bubbles and Other Questions about Science, by Barbara Taylor (Kingfisher Books)

What Makes Popcorn Pop?: And Other Questions about the World around Us, edited by Jack Myers (Boyds Mills Press)

The *Magic School Bus* series (Scholastic)

FRIENDS

For Parents and Children Together

Winnie the Pooh, and other books written by A. A. Milne and illustrated by E. A. Sheppard (Dutton Children's Books)

When the Sun Rose, by Barbara Helen Berger (Philomel Books)

Corduroy, by Don Freeman (Puffin Books)

For Beginning Readers

A Letter for Amy, and other books by Ezra Jack Keats (Viking Press)

Arthur's Eyes, and other books by Marc Brown (Atlantic Monthly Press/ Little, Brown and Co.)

Best Friends, by Stephen Kellogg (E. P. Dutton)

Frog and Toad series, by Arnold Lobel (HarperCollins Publishers)

Leo, Zack, and Emmy, by Amy Ehrlich. Illustrated by Steven Kellogg (Dial Press)

For Independent Readers

Harriet the Spy, by Louise Fitzhugh (HarperCollins Children's Books)

ACTIVE PLAY

For Parents and Children Together

Sharing Nature with Children, by Joseph Cornell (Dawn Publications)

Owl Moon, by Jane Yolen. Illustrated by John Schoenherr (Philomel Books)

Trumpet of the Swan and other books by E. B. White (HarperCollins Juvenile Books)

Peter Rabbit and other books by Beatrix Potter (Warne)

Playing Right Field, by Willy Welch. Illustrated by Marc Simont (Scholastic)

For Beginning Readers

Anna Banana: 101 Jumprope Rhymes, by Joanna Cole. Illustrated by Alan Tiegreen (William Morrow and Co.)

For Independent Readers

Catcher with a Glass Arm, and other books by Matt Christopher (Little, Brown and Co.)

CREATIVE PLAY

For Parents and Children Together

The Art Lesson, by Tomie de Paola (Paper Star)

Easy Origami, by Kazuo Kobayashi, Nihon Vogue, Chihara Sunayama, and Keiko Hori. Edited by Jane Laferia (Lark Books)

Abiyoyo, by Pete Seeger. Illustrated by Michael Hays (Macmillan)

I See the Rhythm, by Toyomi Igus and Michele Wood (Children's Book Press)

Shake It to the One That You Love the Best: Play Songs and Lullabies from Black Musical Traditions. Edited by Cheryl W. Mattox. Illustrated by Brenda Joysmith (JTG of Nashville)

Lotions, Potions, and Slime: Mudpies and More, by Nancy Blakey. Illustrated by Melissah Watts (Tricycle Press)

The Ultimate Book of Kid Concoctions: More Than 65 Wacky, Wild & Crazy Concoctions, by John E. Thomas and Danita Pagel (Kid Concoctions Co.)

Cooking Wizardry for Kids, by Margaret Kenda and Phyllis S. Williams (Barrons Juveniles)

The Kids' Multicultural Cookbook : Food & Fun Around the World, by Deanna F. Cook. Illustrated by Michael P. Kline (Williamson Publishing)

For Beginning Readers
Green Eggs and Ham, by Dr. Seuss (Random House)

For Independent Readers
The Bobbsey Twins series, by Laura Lee Hope. Illustrated by Pepe Gonzalez (Price Stern Sloan Publishers)

Big Top Recipes for Little People: The Big Apple Circus Official Cookbook for Kids and Would-Be Clowns (Favorite Recipes Press)

PRETEND PLAY

For Parents and Children Together
And to Think That I Saw It on Mulberry Street, by Dr. Seuss (Random House)

If You Give a Moose a Cookie, by Laura Joffe Numeroff. Illustrated by Felicia Bond (HarperCollins)

Little Fox Goes to the End of the World, by Ann Tompert. Illustrated by John Wallner (Scholastic)

Tar Beach, by Faith Ringgold (Crown)

Three Tales of My Father's Dragon, by Ruth Stiles Gannett. Illustrated by Ruth Chrisman Gannett (Random House)

For Beginning Readers
Cloudy with a Chance of Meatballs, by Judi Barrett. Illustrated by Ron Barrett (Macmillan)

Kofi and His Magic, by Maya Angelou. Photographs by Margaret Courtney-Clarke (Clarkson Potter)

For Independent Readers
American Girl Collection (Pleasant Company Publications)

Charlie and the Chocolate Factory (Puffin), and other books by Roald Dahl

Strega Nona, by Tomie de Paola (Simon and Schuster)

The True Story of the Three Little Pigs, by A. Wolf, by Jon Scieszka. Illustrated by Lane Smith (Puffin)

SCHOOL PLAY

For Parents and Children Together

Timothy Goes to School, by Rosemary Wells (E. P. Dutton)

When Will I Read?: Welcome to First Grade, by Miriam Cohen. Illustrated by Lillian Hoban (Bantam Doubleday Dell Publishing)

Will I Have a Friend?, by Miriam Cohen. Illustrated by Lillian Hoban (Aladdin Paperbacks)

Hooray for Diffendoofer Day!, by Jack Prelutsky. Illustrated by Lane Smith. Based on a story concept and sketches by Theodore Giesel (Dr. Seuss) (Knopf)

A Call to Character: A Family Treasury of Stories, Poems, Plays, Proverbs, and Fables to Guide the Development of Values for You and Your Children, edited by Colin Greer and Herbert Kohl (HarperCollins)

A House Is a House for Me, by Mary Ann Hoberman. Illustrated by Betty Fraser (Viking Press)

A Light in the Attic, by Shel Silverstein (HarperCollins Juvenile Books)

One Grain of Rice: A Mathematical Folktale, by Demi (Scholastic)

Bet You Can and *Bet You Can't,* by Vicki Cobb and Kathy Darling (Avon Books)

Jumanji, by Chris Van Allsburg (Houghton Mifflin)

For Beginning Readers

A Chocolate Moose for Dinner, by Fred Gwynne (Aladdin Paperbacks)

Amelia Bedelia, and other books by Peggy Parish. Illustrated by Fritz Siebel (HarperCollins Juvenile Books)

Miss Nelson Is Missing, and other books by Harry Allard and James Marshall (Houghton Mifflin)

Morris Goes to School, by B. Wiseman (HarperCollins Children's Books)

One Fish Two Fish Red Fish Blue Fish, and other books by Dr. Seuss (Random House)

For Independent Readers

Angel Child, Dragon Child, by Michele Surat (Scholastic)

How Much is a Million?, by David Schwartz. Illustrated by Stephen Kellogg
(William Morrow and Co.)

Math Curse, by Jon Scieszka. Illustrated by Lane Smith (Viking Children's
Books)

FAMILY

For Parents and Children Together

Abuela, by Arthur Dorros. Illustrated by Elisa Kleven (Puffin)

Alexander and the Terrible, Horrible, No Good, Very Bad Day, and other books
by Judith Viorst. Illustrated by Ray Cruz (Atheneum)

The *Mrs. Piggle-Wiggle* series, by Betty MacDonald. Illustrated by Hilary
Knight (Harper Trophy)

The Keeping Quilt, by Patricia Polacco (Simon and Schuster)

For Beginning Readers

A Birthday for Francis, and other books by Russell and Lillian Hoban
(Harper Trophy)

Much Bigger than Martin, by Steven Kellogg (Dial Books for Young
Readers)

A Chair for My Mother, by Vera B. Williams (Greenwillow Books)

For Independent Readers

Beezus and Ramona, and other books by Beverly Cleary (William Morrow
and Co.)

The One in the Middle Is a Green Kangaroo, and other books by Judy Blume
(Dell Publishing)

Acknowledgments

This book is a collaborative effort.

WENDY MASI, PH.D., Director of the Family Center at Nova Southeastern University, is our toughest critic. She raked through the manuscript with a fine-tooth comb and weeded out passages that were inaccurate or unclear.

ANN MCELWAIN, M.B.A., Director of Marketing and Product Development at the Family Center at Nova Southeastern University, assumed the major responsibility for implementing the photo sessions. She has an uncanny way of convincing children to do the right thing at the right time.

SUZANNE GREGORY, Marilyn's most valuable assistant, deciphered our handwriting and incorporated volumes of new material and rewrites into a manageable manuscript.

THE STAFF OF THE UNIVERSITY SCHOOL OF NOVA SOUTHEASTERN UNIVERSITY participated in focus groups discussing the social play of five-to-eight-year-old students and provided us with the opportunity to observe and photograph the children on the playground.

THE PARENTS of the children featured in this book participated in lengthy interviews, sharing their favorite anecdotes, and providing insightful descriptions of their children's play, questions, favorite activities, explorations, and creative expressions.

Index

About the Authors

MARILYN SEGAL, PH.D., a developmental psychologist specializing in early childhood, is professor of human development and dean emeritus of the Family and School Center at Nova Southeastern University in Fort Lauderdale, Florida. The mother of five children, she is the author of nineteen books, including *Making Friends*, *Just Pretending*, and this five-volume series, *Your Child at Play*. She is also the creator of *To Reach a Child*, a nine-part television series for parents, and *In Time and With Love*, a book for parents of young children with special needs.

BETTY BARDIGE, ED.D., is developmental psychologist, educator, and curriculum designer. She has authored numerous computer-based books for young readers, including more than twenty titles in the comprehensive Tapestry series. She has also written for parents and teachers. She currently chairs the A. L. Mailman Family Foundation, a national early childhood fund that promotes high-quality child care, family support, and education that fosters social responsibility. Betty is the daughter of Marilyn Segal and the mother of Kori, Brenan, and Arran Bardige.

PARENTING/CHILDCARE BOOKS FROM NEWMARKET PRESS

Ask for these titles at your local bookstore or use this coupon and enclose a check or money order payable to: **Newmarket Press**, 18 East 48th Street, New York, NY 10017.

Amelia D. Auckett
Baby Massage
_____ $11.95 pb (1-55704-022-2)

Elissa P. Benedek, M.D., and Catherine F. Brown, M.Ed.
How to Help Your Child Overcome Your Divorce
_____ $14.95 pb (1-55704-329-9)

Lee F. Gruzen
Raising Your Jewish/Christian Child
_____ $14.95 pb (1-55704-059-1)

Debra W. Haffner, M.P.H.
From Diapers to Dating: A Parent's Guide to Raising Sexually Healthy Children
_____ $23.95 hc (1-55704-385-X)

Sally Placksin
Mothering the New Mother, Rev. Ed.
_____ $16.95 pb (1-55704-317-5)

Teresa Savage
The Ready-to-Read, Ready-to-Count Handbook
_____ $11.95 pb (1-55704-093-1)

Dan Schaefer & Christine Lyons
How Do We Tell the Children? Updated Ed.
_____ $18.95 hc (1-55704-189-X)
_____ $11.95 pb (1-55704-181-4)

Adriane G. Berg & Arthur Berg Bochner
The Totally Awesome Business Book for Kids
_____ $10.95 pb (1-55704-226-8)
The Totally Awesome Money Book for Kids (and Their Parents)
_____ $10.95 pb (1-55704-176-8)

Frederick Leboyer, M.D.
Inner Beauty, Inner Light: Yoga for Pregnant Women
_____ $18.95 pb (1-55704-315-9)
Loving Hands: Traditional Baby Massage
_____ $16.95 pb (1-55704-314-0)

Lynda Madaras & Area Madaras
My Body, My Self for Boys
_____ $11.95 pb (1-55704-230-6)
My Body, My Self for Girls
_____ $11.95 pb (1-55704-150-4)
My Feelings, My Self
_____ $11.95 pb (1-55704-157-1)
The What's Happening to My Body? Book for Boys
_____ $18.95 hc (1-55704-002-8)
_____ $11.95 pb (0-937858-99-4)
The What's Happening to My Body? Book for Girls
_____ $18.95 hc (1-55704-001-X)
_____ $11.95 pb (0-937858-98-6)

Robert Schwebel, Ph.D.
How to Help Your Kids Choose to Be Tobacco-Free
_____ $19.95 hc (1-55704-368-X)
Saying No Is Not Enough, Rev. Ed.
_____ $14.95 pb (1-55704-318-3)

Marilyn Segal, Ph.D.
In Time and With Love
_____ $21.95 hc (0-937858-95-1)
_____ $15.95 pb (0-937858-96-X)
Your Child at Play: Birth to One Year, 2nd Ed.
_____ $27.95 hc (1-55704-334-5)
_____ $17.95 pb (1-55704-330-2)
Your Child at Play: One to Two Years, 2nd Ed.
_____ $27.95 hc (1-55704-335-3)
_____ $16.95 pb (1-55704-331-0)
Your Child at Play: Two to Three Years, 2nd Ed.
_____ $27.95 hc (1-55704-336-1)
_____ $16.95 pb (1-55704-332-9)
Your Child at Play: Three to Five Years, 2nd Ed.
_____ $27.95 hc (1-55704-337-X)
_____ $16.95 pb (1-55704-337-7)
Your Child at Play: Five to Eight Years
_____ $27.95 hc (1-55704-402-3)
_____ $17.95 pb (1-55704-401-5)

For postage and handling, please add $3.00 for the first book, plus $1.00 for each additional book. Prices and availability are subject to change.

I enclose a check or money order payable to **Newmarket Press** in the amount of $ _____

Name _____

Address _____

City/State/Zip _____

For discounts on orders of five or more copies or to get a catalog, contact Newmarket Press, Special Sales Department, 18 East 48th Street, New York, NY 10017; phone 212-832-3575 or 800-669-3903; fax 212-832-3629; or e-mail newmktprs@aol.com.